ST DOMINIC

ST DOMINIC

A Pictorial Biography

by

Leonard von Matt
and Marie-Humbert Vicaire, O.P.

Translated from the French by
Gerard Meath, O.P.

HENRY REGNERY COMPANY

Chicago

This Edition first published in 1957
Henry Regnery Company
64 East Jackson Blvd.
Chicago 4, Illinois

© Longmans, Green and Co. Ltd. 1957

PLATES PRINTED BY IMAGO, ZÜRICH, TEXT PRINTED IN GREAT
BRITAIN BY HAZELL WATSON AND VINEY LTD., AYLESBURY AND
SLOUGH. NIHIL OBSTAT: ANDREAS MOORE, L.C.L. CENSOR
DEPUTATUS. IMPRIMATUR: ✠ GEORGIUS L. CRAVEN, EPŪS
SEBASTOPOLIS, V.G. WESTMONASTERII, DIE 9A SEPTEMBER 1957

CONTENTS

ACKNOWLEDGMENTS

Illustrations, presentation and general design: Leonard von Matt, Buochs, Switzerland. All the photographs were taken by him during 1956 specially for this book, with the exception of the following which were derived from the sources named: Plate 7, Patrimonio Nacional, Madrid; Plate 28, Library of Basel University; Plates 54, 108, 129, 133, 137, 138, 156, Alinari, Florence; Plate 107, Mas, Barcelona; Plates 109–117, Biblioteca Apostolica Vaticana; Plate 156, Villani, Bologna; Plate 158, Bologna University; Plate 159, The Fogg Art Museum, Harvard University, Cambridge, Mass., U.S.A.

Text: Marie-Humbert Vicaire, O.P., Professor of Church History in the University of Fribourg. The author does not refer to his authorities or literary sources; these will be found fully set out in the two works which he was writing at the same time as the present text and which are complementary to it: *Saint Dominique de Caleruega, d'après les documents du XIIIe siècle* (Paris, Les éditions du Cerf, 1955), and *Histoire de saint Dominique*, 2 vols. (Paris, Les éditions du Cerf, 1957).

Map: Sebastian Bullough, O.P.

This English translation, based on the original French, is issued by arrangement with NZN Buchverlag, Zürich, publishers of the original German edition of which separate editions are issued in Western Germany and Austria.
This work appears also in French, Italian, Dutch, Spanish and Portuguese editions.

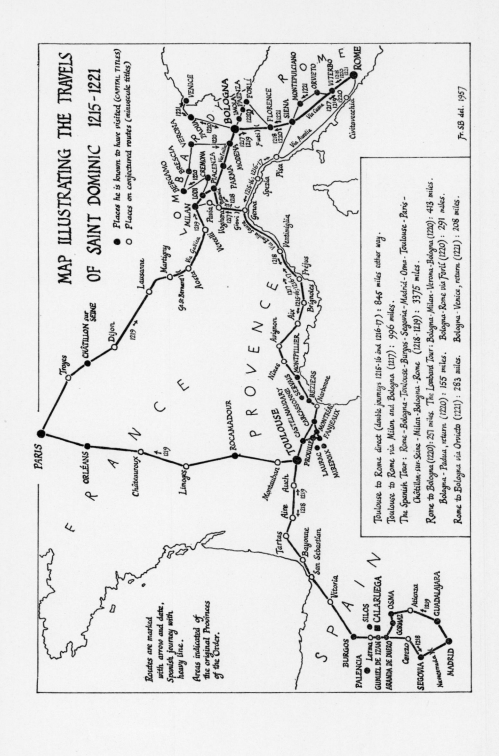

MAP ILLUSTRATING THE TRAVELS OF SAINT DOMINIC 1215-1221

ROMAN SPAIN

SAINT DOMINIC'S roots lay in Spain on the high plateau of Old Castile. It is a land steeped in history; largely the Spain of the Roman Empire. Following the course of the Duero the Roman legions laid their imperial highways from Tarragona to Corunna, from the Mediterranean coast to the Atlantic. Starting at Saragossa, the chief highway ran through Numantia, Olbega, Osma; at Clunia it forked, the route through Róa and Simancas leading to Zamora, and that through Palencia going to Astorga and the sea-coast. This spot at Clunia was only a few miles from Caleruega, the birthplace of St Dominic. Set high on a great hill, this powerful city was by the twelfth century little more than a heap of stones. But the villages that had grown up around it and the extent of the ruins, which must have held within their confines from sixty to eighty thousand inhabitants, bore witness to the splendour of the deserted camp and the deep impression made by the Roman settlers. The great roads still usable in the middle ages, with their main artery running only a few miles from Caleruega, led to other cities and settlements and spread in a network over the ancient land of Iberia. The high broad walls, the mosaics, the crumbling pillars and the paving stones of the roads where Roman chariot wheels had worn grooves for nearly a thousand years, could all tell countless tales to the children of mediaeval Spain. They could speak of human greatness and Christian dignity; for Christianity, too, had found its place among the Roman inheritance. Bishoprics had been set up and the long glorious story of the Church in Spain was begun. Almost all the cities that figured in St Dominic's life—Osma, Róa, Palencia, Segovia—had, like the roads he trod, staff in hand, been touched by Roman civilisation.

ROMAN SPAIN
Notes on the three plates that follow:

1 THE ROMAN BRIDGE ACROSS THE UCERO ON THE WAY
INTO OSMA
The ancient Uxuma Argelae Arevacorum was taken over first by the Romans and then by
the Visigoths because of its important strategic position at the crossroads. At the end of the
sixth century it became an episcopal see (Oxoma). At the top of the hill by the roadside can
be seen the feudal fortifications guarding the approach to the mediaeval *burgo* and the ancient
castrum.

2 "EL PUENTE", THE NOBLE ROMAN AQUEDUCT OF SEGOVIA
Built in the reign of Augustus, it is the largest of the ancient aqueducts which have survived
to modern times. It is 796 yards long. Through the first two arches can be seen the towers of
two romanesque churches, gems of the town, which Dominic himself must have seen in 1219.

3 THE HERMITAGE OF "NOSTRA SEÑORA DE CASTRO" ON THE
SITE OF ANCIENT CLUNIA
For centuries this spot has been the object of pilgrimage from Caleruega, the birthplace of
St Dominic. One of the last surviving links between country and town perpetuated by
Christianity. In the foreground are the remains of a Roman house of Clunia unearthed by
recent excavations.

[2]

MOHAMMEDANISM, not old age, had destroyed Clunia and the neighbouring towns. Between 714 and 995, Osma changed hands six times and became frontier-town for now one, now the other, of the warring parties. From the eighth century to the beginning of the eleventh, Clunia was in turn occupied by Alfonso the Catholic, by Gonzalo Fernandez, by Abd-er-Rahman III, by the terrible Al Mansur and finally by Sancho of Castile. During these years the vast uplands watered by the Duero were occupied by Christians or Moham- medans, or else were left for long periods as a kind of no-man's-land, great wastes overrun by contending armies, with no security and scarcely any life. At first, the Christians were hemmed in away from the sea in the Cantabrian Mountains, and made sortie after sortie to recover ground. Then, for more than a century, they were compelled to mark time by the northern edge of the plateau, while they built fortified towers and castles to act as salients and advance posts in what became Castile. At the turn of the eleventh century, they finally went forward above Toledo in a decisive attack, and secured the line of the Tagus for Christian Spain. From then onwards, the cities along the Duero— Róa, Aranda, Osma—securely placed behind the advancing Castilian armies, came to life again. One after another, they prospered through the twelfth century; the population grew, dioceses were re-established, churches came out of hiding. The kings of Castile, with their *ricohombres*, pursued their military campaigns in the South to the bitter end with the Cross as well as the sword, until that day in July 1212 when King Alfonso VIII, with the help of Navarre and Aragon, by his brilliant victory at Las Navas de Tolosa, settled for the next three centuries the southern boundary of the Christian lands reclaimed from the Moslems.

Alfonso was the contemporary of Dominic, and such was the spirit of restoration, youth and vigorous crusading for the faith of Christ, in Castile and the valley of the Duero, when Dominic was born.

"RECONQUISTA"

Notes on the seven plates that follow:

4   THE MOZARABIC HERMITAGE OF SAN BAUDELIO

Situated just under sixteen miles to the south-west of Osma, its arches of Moorish origin show the influence and no doubt the handiwork of the Moorish craftsmen who remained in the country after the re-conquest. This remote church is a Christian building of the eleventh century, sign of the victory of the Cross.

5   INLAID JEWELLED CROSS FROM SILOS

This cross, kept at the Benedictine abbey of Silos, twelve miles north of Caleruega, was carried by the Christian knights in their wars against the Moors.

6   SWORD AND SPURS OF A CASTILIAN KING AT THE TIME OF THE RE-CONQUEST

Observe the regular pattern of Moorish design which adorns the scabbard of the sword, and by contrast the small inlaid cross in the steel blade. (*Musée des armes de Madrid.*)

7   THE STANDARD OF LAS NAVAS DE TOLOSA

The Moors went to war bearing standards like this. This one, which is preserved at the monastery of Las Huelgas near Burgos, was captured in 1212 at the famous victory of Las Navas.

8   BY CROSS AND SWORD

The seal of King St Ferdinand III of Castile (1217–1230). On their seals the kings of this period liked to be depicted on horseback, carrying a shield and brandishing a sword. This warlike spirit gained lustre from the ideal of Spanish chivalry which reached its peak in the re-conquest. (*Archivio historico nacional, Madrid.*)

9   THE VALLEY OF THE DUERO

The whole character of Castile is depicted here: the broad bed of the river, almost dried up; the arches of the mediaeval bridge; a small settlement nestling against the parched hillside scarred with ravines and ravaged by the wind; at the top a strong tower like the *torreón* of Caleruega.

10   SOUTH WALL OF THE CASTLE OF PEÑAFIEL

This vast fortress, covering the entire hill, rises up to the south of the Duero fifty miles west of Caleruega. The Infante Manuel made it his headquarters and built near it a fine Dominican priory as a resting-place for the body of St Dominic's mother.

[4]

SAINT DOMINIC's early biographers speak only very briefly of the family from which he sprang. "His father was called Felix, his mother Jane." They were married in 1170. A rather more recent biographer states emphatically that Dominic's father was a person of importance in the village, and a landowner. He was able to give his children the best education. Dominic and his brothers received the tonsure and attended ths echools, which in the twelfth century was very rare.

A collection of documents and traditions concerning Caleruega from the thirteenth to the fifteenth century, found both in Italy and in Spain, provides the explanation. Dominic's father was the "squire" of his village and undoubtedly owned the "land of Don Felix" of which a contemporary document speaks. The family combined the privileges of two noble Castilian lines. Caleruega, a village of independent origin, was governed by the feudal system called *behetría*, and by tradition this government was always in the hands of a member of the Aza family, one of the oldest in the country, and the family from which Jane, Dominic's mother, came. When Felix Guzmán married Jane, the other ancient family of the district was united to that of Aza, and together they became the suzerains whom Caleruega could choose as rulers. The names Aza and Guzmán were to become famous in the middle ages, and were already so by the end of the twelfth century, especially the name of Aza. Both the families were *ricohombres* of Castile, privileged to bear the title *Don*; they signed royal charters side by side with bishops, assisted the kings in their military campaigns and government, and took a full part in initiating and carrying out the re-conquest of Spain from the Moors. Their horizon had now extended to the frontiers of Castile. The generosity, bravery, enterprise and daring, the high tradition of service to King and Church which we find in Dominic, were all part of his birthright.

This people's manner of life was of the simplest. They were soldiers, either on the road and in action, or else living simply among their peasants;

their lives were divided between the field of battle and the field of work. It is possible to imagine their way of life by recalling the feudal "mounds" in which they camped with their sergeants in the twelfth century. They were lonely towers on the top of some prominence, with no ditch or fortification, protected merely by a fence. Such was the headquarters of the squire of Caleruega.

TWO NOBLE FAMILIES

Notes on the four plates that follow:

11   GUZMÁN

The estate of the family to which St Dominic's father belonged is to-day a village of agricultural workers. The castle has disappeared. The picture shows some of the inhabitants busy making bricks with a mixture of clay and straw. In the countryside of Castile, just as in St Dominic's time, the peasants still build houses and barns with bricks made from clay dried in the sun.

12   THE SMALL FORTIFIED TOWN OF AZA

Nineteen miles from Caleruega and Guzmán and to the south of the Duero whose valley it overlooks. The strong feudal buildings in fine freestone contrast with the poverty of the present-day village. They were not so important, but were already of considerable age, when Jane of Aza married Felix of Guzmán in 1170. Half-way up the hill are the *bodegas*, cellars hollowed out of the limestone. In these the peasants of the region store the red wine with which they quench their thirst, drinking it from leather bottles as they work in the fields.

13   TWO PEASANT GIRLS OF AZA

Hard work with the hoe and sheep-raising were the two commonest occupations of a peasant's life in Castile in the middle ages.

14   SAINT PAUL OF PEÑAFIEL

This old Dominican church was built by the Infante Don Juan Manuel about 1340 to house the body of St Dominic's mother, Jane of Aza. She herself was beatified by the Church in 1834. This renaissance window is obviously of later date than the actual church building.

DOMINIC'S BIRTH

CALERUEGA was not a hundred years old when Dominic was born there between 1171 and 1173. As the population increased, this village sprang into existence on a plateau half-way up a hill. It had only been a parish for thirty or forty years, and the romanesque parish church, its newly carved stones still gleaming white, seemed to burst with new life and proclaim its youth.

At the highest point of the plateau, on a slight spur, stood a squat four-sided tower commanding all the roads which debouched into the valley below. This was the *torreón*, the home of the squire, father of St Dominic; but he was not born here among soldiers in an unfriendly barracks. About a hundred yards away, a chapel marks the site of the house in which he was born. A godmother of noble birth took him to church, and the font in which he was baptised is still preserved to-day.

Many witnesses claimed to have seen a light shining over his forehead while he was still a child; no doubt this came from the light of grace that entered his soul at baptism. Even at the end of his life the "kind of luminous splendour" which shone from his forehead, and seemed to filter through his closed eyelids when he was praying, "won everybody's respect and love". Was this just the limpid look of a pure affectionate child, or was it already that special supernatural grace of the saint whose complete assurance in following Christ and his Apostles serves "to enlighten them that sit in darkness and in the shadow of death"?

Certainly his mother had borne this baby in a deep religious spirit, and from the first days of his conception had offered him in her heart to the service of God. History cherishes the memory of Jane's great gift of compassion, and she undoubtedly passed on to her son her own acute sensitiveness to other people's sorrows and to everyone's suffering.

DOMINIC'S BIRTH

Notes on the four plates that follow:

15 THE FONT AT CALERUEGA IN WHICH DOMINIC WAS BAPTISED

It is a simple romanesque bowl cut out of stone. The kings of Spain, descended from the Guzmáns, wished to have their children baptised in it. It was taken to Valladolid for Philip II's baptism and later to Madrid, where the Sisters, whom Dominic established there, preserve it in its silver casing.

16 THE *TORREÓN* OF CALERUEGA

This tower is not entirely ancient. The upper part, the battlements, the door with its two escutcheons, the three steps and the staircase date from 1952 to 1955. The double window, with the small lightly decorated (*mudéjar*) romanesque column, would date from the twelfth century, when a rough door was cut in the wall at ground level to render habitable what had been a defensive "mound" in the tenth and eleventh centuries. Originally the tower ended in a wooden defence gallery, supported from the stone corbels which still remain and reached by the apertures on the second storey.

17 CALERUEGA SEEN FROM THE HILL OF SAINT GEORGE

In the centre is the parish church. Behind the belfry is the *torreón* surrounded by the quadrangle of a newly constructed hostelry (1952–1955). To the left is the cloister of the Dominican Sisters built by Alfonso X of Castile in 1266. The chapel marking St Dominic's birthplace is to the left of the Sisters' convent. In the background lie the uplands of the Duero valley, visible as far as the Sierra de Guadarrama, forty-seven miles away.

18 THE PARISH CHURCH OF SAINT LAURENCE

The nave is modern and the portico with its columns contemporary. But the door, whose romanesque columns lie beneath the portico, the belfry and the apse, which may be seen in the preceding picture, are of the mid-twelfth century. The hill or *peña* of St George is 3,270 feet above sea-level, which gives some indication of the harshness of the climate. On the hillsides are the *bodegas* of the village.

[8]

CHILDHOOD AT CALERUEGA

As the little boys of Caleruega still do to-day, Dominic often climbed the hill at the end of the village to play and spy out the land. There used to be a chapel of St George on that spot, but there is now no trace of it. As he looked north, he would see the high peaks of the Iberian Mountains, black in the summer, white with snow in winter. As he looked south and west, he would see the vast bleak stretch of Old Castile.

What did the young Dominic see as he turned his solemn eyes towards the endless horizon? The labours, sufferings and sorrows of men? The workmen below, hauling the limestone to the kiln from which the village gets its name? The old women sitting outside their homes, spinning and twisting wool with their skilful fingers? The farm labourers hacking the earth, parched and hardened by the over-long summer? Or the shepherds who, as far as the eye could see, tended their huge flocks from which the village drew a living? At nightfall, as the flocks returned to their folds, he would hear their murmur growing louder and louder as they drew near to him, the bleating confused, insistent, endless, as they made towards food, rest and quiet in a safe shelter.

Spread over the plain, but hidden in the folds of the hillsides, the boy could picture innumerable men labouring in villages like Caleruega; farther off beyond the sierras, Christian soldiers face to face with Moslems; farther off still, other Christians, their faith on trial in Moslem prisons; then the pagans themselves imprisoned in their heresy; and finally, all over the world, countless men, prisoners of ignorance and sin. These were his human fellows; and their cries, like those of the flocks, reached his rock above Caleruega, speaking to him of their longings, their hopes and their vast need of the truth which makes men free.

CHILDHOOD AT CALERUEGA

Notes on the four plates that follow:

19 THE SOLEMN, MANLY EXPRESSION OF A YOUNG SPANIARD

20 THE ROMANESQUE CHURCH OF ESPINOSA SHELTERED BEHIND
THE HILL

This church is contemporary with the church at Caleruega, its neighbour to the south. It
provides refuge for the people as it does for the magpies and storks which have nested in the
belfry for eight centuries.

21 AN OLD WOMAN SPINNING

22 THE ''CALERA'' OR TRADITIONAL LIME KILN

It is similar to the one which gave its name to Caleruega, the "small lime kiln".

[10]

THE name Dominic means "The Man of God". A tall order for a boy! But the name was not uncommon in that district nor in the village itself. Caleruega came under the control of the abbey of Silos, and only a century earlier in 1073 the great reformer of the abbey, another Dominic, had died renowned for holiness.

Twenty-five miles north of Caleruega, in the heart of the Iberian Mountains, lay this Visigoth abbey restored by the famous Fernand Gonzalez who had begun in this area his re-Christianising of the upper valley of the Duero. More than most, this abbey had escaped the Moslem depredations. It was naturally protected by its position on a steep spur, and in the middle of the eleventh century had been restored by Abbot Dominic, who began at once to build a superb monastery. Since the death of the holy abbot, the pilgrims who gathered here from all over the country spread stories of the holiness of the monks and the fame of their reformer. Dominic's parents and the boy himself would not fail to make their own pilgrimage. Caleruega itself stood at the head of the road to Silos.

The village did not come under the influence of this abbey alone. It was also closely associated with the monastery of St Peter, founded in 1073 at Gumiel de Izan downstream on the river which ran at the base of the *torreón*. While Dominic was still a child, the monastery was given over to the Cistercians from Fitero-Caletrava, and thus there was planted in the district the contemplative Order of Saint Bernard and the military Order of Christian Knighthood.

Fifteen miles to the south-east there was a third abbey, Our Lady of La Vid. Here lived the Canons Regular of Prémontre of the strict observance, who from 1152 onwards had blessed the district with their ministry and holy lives. The cathedral chapter of Osma (1136), and the collegiate chapters of Róa and Soria (1152), likewise brought the Augustinian Canons into the district. Notice the dates of all these foundations. Like the diocese, the romanesque chapels and the villages themselves, these monasteries were in the full vigour of their youth when St Dominic was born.

[11]

THE SPLENDOUR OF THE CLOISTER
Notes on the four plates that follow:

23 SITE OF THE ABBEY OF SAINT PETER OF GUMIEL
This abbey of black monks ,seven or eight miles to the west of Caleruega, inhabited by black monks for the first century of its existence, was taken over in 1194 by the chaplains of the Order of Caletrava, an ancient foundation of Cistercians from the abbey of Fitero. After the expulsion of the monks in the nineteenth century, the deserted buildings gradually fell into decay. Only the cloister walls remain, enclosing fertile fields in a land of thin pasturage—a reminder of the quality of the work of the white monks.

24 THE ROMANESQUE MADONNA OF THE BENEDICTINES OF SILOS

25 THE PRE-ROMANESQUE CLOISTER OF SAINT DOMINIC OF SILOS
Begun in the middle of the eleventh century when Cluny was restoring the Church in Spain, and continued throughout the following century, this jewel of Spanish monasticism reflects the glory of the monks at the end of the twelfth century. Re-built eight centuries later by monks of Solesmes, the abbey is now spreading the best traditions of plain-chant throughout the country.

26 SAN JUAN DE DUERO
Remarkable ruins of a house of the Knights Templars to the east of Soria.

[12]

ABOUT the age of seven, Dominic left his family and his home. His parents had dedicated him to the Church. His uncle, the archpriest, would provide his education, presumably in his own church, for the training of a young priest anywhere outside the church was unthinkable. In the middle of the choir, among scholars of his own age, Dominic learnt from the manuscript psalter to read and to sing psalms. In the house of the cloister near by, he was introduced to writing, grammar and the problems of simple arithmetic.

At the age of fourteen, it was time to go to the schools. The best ones were at Palencia. There ten years would be devoted to the humanities, dialectic and then theology. At this time the New Testament, of which he knew substantial passages by heart, was his staple reading. After the fashion of the time, he unravelled the difficulties of the scriptures with the help of the commentaries of the Fathers, which he copied into the margin of his parchment Bible. At the same time, by discussion and questions he delved into the deeper meaning of Holy Writ. In this manner his knowledge of the Gospels became clear and deep.

Reserved as he was by temperament, he spent long hours alone. He was free to organise his own time-table, and day by day he increased his periods of study and especially of prayer. But these hours of silence and solitude did not cause him to turn in upon himself. On the contrary he grew more conscious of the sufferings of his neighbours, the mere thought of which was sufficient to cloud his clear, open countenance.

During a long famine, he did not hesitate to sell everything he possessed, including the precious books annotated in his own hand. "How can I study on dead skins," he said, "while the poor are dying of hunger?" He founded an alms-house where the starving people came daily for help.

So, when he had sold or given away everything he possessed, he was not content until he had given his very self to the poor in Christ.

A PRIEST'S TRAINING

Notes on the five plates that follow:

27   ARANDA DE DUERO

It is not known where Dominic's uncle, the archpriest, lived. In the neighbourhood of Caleruega in the middle ages, archpriests lived at Aranda de Duero, Aza and Róa. The nearest, fourteen miles away, was Aranda, and this picture shows its mediaeval bridge over the Duero and a small thirteenth-century church.

28   THEOLOGICAL TEACHING IN THE TWELFTH CENTURY: "QUESTIONS IN DIVINITY"

The bishop is Gilbert de la Porrée (Poitiers, 1142–1154), pressed by his disciples into undertaking the study of the theology of Boethius. Notice the dove from heaven, a symbol of inspiration, the master's halo and the animation of the students, one of whom is little more than a child. (*Manuscript from the library of Basel.*)

29   TWO SEALS OF BISHOPS OF PALENCIA

On the left, that of Alderico (?1208); on the right, that of Tello (1211–1240), under whose rule the schools of Palencia became a university.

30   SEAL OF THE BISHOP OF OSMA, MARTIN BAZAN (1189–1201)

The bishop who received Dominic into his cathedral chapter. The inscription *Martinus Dei gratia Essomensis episcopus* emphasises the independence of the diocese at this time. The bishop did not receive nomination from the King but was elected by the Canons.

31   "SAINT DOMINIC'S MULBERRY TREE" AT PALENCIA

The garden of *Hermanitas de los ancianos de Lamparados*, where this tree is situated, belonged to a house recently destroyed. St Dominic was said to have lodged there, but its architecture makes this unlikely.

[14]

THE CHAPTER OF OSMA

IN 1196 Dominic joined the cathedral chapter of Osma and returned to the heart of his own diocese. Don Diego de Azévèdo, the Prior of the chapter, took good care not to miss the services of such an apostle, and had obtained the consent of the bishop, Martin Bazan, to bring Dominic into the community.

The mediaeval township, where Dominic was to live for ten years, no longer stood on the site of the ancient town of Oxoma. The old town had stood high on a steep rock; the new town lay near the waters of the Avion and Ucero, ringed with hills. Sheltered among heavily leaved trees, the town and its cathedral were wrapped in peace. The romanesque church, not fifty years old, stood out fresh and newly built. The diocese itself was scarcely any older, for it had been restored in 1110 by St Peter of Bourges, who had been a monk of Cluny, and the power of the prayer and love of the holy man was still felt in the diocese.

Beside the cathedral itself stood the monastery cloister, and on one side are still to be seen three doorways with semicircular arches and gryphons on the capitals, through which Dominic must have passed many times. A vaulted passage-way leads off through the door of the convent, and through this the new postulant went on his way to give himself to the life of prayer. On either side of a walled-up door there stand twin windows with rounded arches and twisted columns; these looked on to the chapter house where, soon after his admission, Dominic assumed the twelfth-century uniform of the Canons Regular, the white tunic and black cloak and hood that can still be seen in the effigies over the tomb of Peter of Osma. This is the habit the Dominicans now wear.

A few months after his profession as a Canon, an important event altered his whole life. He became a priest. Then began that intercourse with God which, unlike many priests of his time, Dominic made a daily event, the offering of Mass. For him this experience was so overpowering that he frequently wept, and "tear followed tear ceaselessly".

THE CHAPTER OF OSMA

Notes on the four plates that follow:

32   A YOUNG DOMINICAN

Echard conjectured that the habit that Dominic gave to his preachers at the foundation of the Order was the one he had received at Osma and continued to wear. For the white tunic this is indisputable. The tomb of St Peter of Osma (cf. fig. 41) shows this to have been also true of the black cappa. The cut of the Dominican habit has altered slightly over the centuries, especially that of the capuce, which has become detached from the scapular and cappa to which it originally belonged, and has developed into a sort of mozzetta.

33   ONE OF THE WINDOWS OF THE CHAPTER HOUSE IN DOMINIC'S TIME

The ornamental capital on the right shows the last Supper, the sacrament of unity and the Washing of the Feet—the *mandatum* of Jesus—which the Canons Regular frequently re-enacted in chapter as a sacramental of brotherly love.

34   THE CLOISTER OF THE CHAPTER AT OSMA

The three doors in the right-hand wall are romanesque. In the foreground is the walled-up door of the chapter house; the double windows which flanked it according to conventual custom were blocked up on this side in the fifteenth century during the construction of the existing gothic cloister.

35   THE TOWN OF OSMA HIDDEN BEHIND A SCREEN OF POPLARS AT THE BOTTOM OF A COOL VALLEY

The *castrum* was on the high hill to the right and out of sight.

[16]

IN 1199 the chapter of Osma reformed and took up full community life. At that time Dominic was sacristan and shortly afterwards became sub-prior. He was deeply devoted to Diego who had now become his bishop (1201) and had attached Dominic to himself. Together they took the great steps which brought about the reform of the community. The success of their work itself speaks more eloquently than any of the many stories told about them.

One hundred and fifty years previously the reformers of the Church had described in burning words the ascetic life of the early Christians in order to bring the clergy back to the full strength of their life of grace. The leading priests of the diocese were the Canons of the chapter, and they filled the role of the twelve Apostles at the centre of the early Church in Jerusalem. They should be like those keen strong shepherds trained by Christ himself: "they lived a common life"; "they had only one heart and one soul"; "no one called anything he had his own"; their time was divided between official prayer in the temple at Jerusalem, preaching to the faithful and others, and the offering of the sacrifice of the Mass in the privacy of their homes: because they were detached from the world, "great grace was given them and they bore witness before men with the greatest possible power to the resurrection of Jesus Christ".

This was the kind of "apostolic life" which the chapter of Osma accepted as their ideal when they were founded in 1136 and began to follow the rule of St Augustine and the traditions of canonical life in community. After a period of falling off, it was the same ideal which they were now steadfastly setting before their eyes again. Dominic gave himself whole-heartedly to the life. He allowed himself to be shaped by the regular life, step by step he followed the Eastern traditions of the Fathers of the desert and the Western customs finding their expression in the chapter of faults. Again he widened and deepened his life of prayer, moving straight from the solemn singing of the divine office in choir to his own private prayers. So eventually, being sub-prior, he came to the work of ministering to souls, for which he had prepared himself with long unflagging prayer for his neighbour, a prayer springing straight from his deep pity and compassion for men.

APOSTOLIC LIFE

Notes on the four plates that follow:

36 DOMINIC'S BOOKS IN THE CHAPTER OF OSMA

The library of the chapter preserves a great number of ancient manuscripts for which there is a catalogue dating from the end of the thirteenth century (the second on the left at the top of the picture). Dominic would have handled many of the manuscripts shown here, without doubt the first on the left in the second and third rows (a fragment on Christ written at the end of the *Moralia* of St Gregory, No. 177c in the library, and the Commentary of Beatus de Liébana on the Apocalypse, dedicated to Eterius of Osma, No. 1). He would certainly have used the last one on the bottom row, a missal of Osma of the end of the twelfth century (No. 165), open in this picture at the illuminated double page which precedes the Canon. It was from this missal that the Saint sang Mass.

37 SAINT DOMINIC: A SMALL FIFTEENTH-CENTURY ALABASTER STATUE

This statue comes from the doorway of the Sisters' convent at Caleruega. Such was the appearance of the Canon of Osma. Hanging from his belt is the knife he normally carried with him.

38 UT SIMUL HABITENT CLERICI: "THAT THE CLERGY MAY LIVE TOGETHER"

The phrase which can be seen at the head of this manuscript, like the illustration, is typical of the spirit of the Rule of St Augustine. Clerics ought to form a community as did their models, the Apostles. (*MS. from Vich.*)

39 THE NEIGHBOURHOOD OF OSMA

Picture taken from the ancient site of the town.

[18]

BEYOND THE PYRENEES

In the spring of 1203, public affairs found their way into Dominic's secluded life, and he began his journeyings over the world. His bishop was sent by Alfonso VIII of Castile on a mission to Denmark, and he took Dominic for his companion.

A marriage was to be arranged, and they were to seek the hand of a foreign princess for the young son of the king, Prince Ferdinand, aged thirteen and a half. Remote, wrapped in the northern mists on the shores of the Baltic, Denmark was yet an important element in the balance of power in Europe, and the King of Castile, like the kings of France and England, had to establish friendly relations there if his foreign policy was to be sound.

The two Castilians set out on horseback with servants and a suitable retinue, crossed the Pyrenees and eventually reached Scandinavia. When the arrangements had been completed they came back to Castile, only to return two years later to Denmark to fetch the girl. But she had died in the meantime and the bishop and his companion did not take the road back to Castile but went to Rome. Serious events were going to cut across their return.

During these four long journeys a whole new world opened before the eyes of the young Canon of Osma. So far Dominic had studied the deep truths of the Gospel and the life of prayer. Now, all over Europe he found himself studying the human panorama of the Church. He saw all her glories: countless churches, powerful bishoprics, widespread religious orders, and in Rome the Pope himself with the Cardinals and the papal court. Innocent III, the head of Christendom, watched over and guided all. Dominic saw too the weaknesses of Christendom: anarchy, ruined churches, wicked cities, the religious problems springing from the shortage of priests, anti-clericalism, ignorance and heresy.

On the north-east borders of Europe he had also found completely pagan districts where there was unlimited scope for Christian missionaries. A great longing sprang up in Dominic's soul, as it did in Diego's, to bring to these lost people the knowledge and love of Christ. Indeed, it was this which drove them both to Rome to ask permission to leave Osma for good and devote themselves henceforward to the conversion of the pagans. The Pope refused, but another mission, equally pressing, awaited the two Castilians.

BEYOND THE PYRENEES

Notes on the five plates that follow:

40 THE LITTLE EPISCOPAL TOWN OF JACA AT THE FOOT OF THE PYRENEES

Diego and Dominic would normally follow the Roman road in the direction of Soria and Saragossa, and then, travelling via Huesca and Jaca, they would come through the pass of Somport to reach the *camino francese* used by pilgrims to Compostella.

41 THE BISHOP OF OSMA TRAVELLING WITH A CANON AND AN ARMED RETAINER (1258)

This carving is found on the tomb of St Peter of Osma in the cathedral and was made less than fifty years after Diego and Dominic were sent by Alfonso VIII on the mission to Denmark. It shows their dress and accoutrement down to the smallest detail, including the horses' harness with large bridle bits. The travellers both wear the same black cape and capuce covering hands and legs. In addition the bishop has a large felt hat. The presence of a foot-soldier indicates that horses were used to lessen fatigue rather than for speed.

42 A HOUSE IN THE PYRENEES NEAR THE SOMPORT PASS

The lumpy chimney-stack covers the rectangular kitchen; a heap of wool dries in the sun after being washed.

43 THE SOMPORT PASS

Not far from the Franco-Spanish border.

44 THE ABBEY CHURCH OF MORLAÁS ON THE TOULOUSE ROAD

Diego's and Dominic's route carried them along the Compostella road with romanesque churches marking the way; one of these near Pau is the abbey church of Morlaás, and the illustration shows the tympanum over the doorway.

DURING their four journeys through the heart of France, the bishop and his companion came face to face with a situation of which until then they had only heard tales. A large part of the county of Toulouse in the province of Narbonne was falling into heresy. One night Dominic discovered that the landlord of the inn where they were lodging was himself abandoning the Faith. In his zeal he could not keep silence, and throughout the night, unmindful of his weariness from a lengthy journey which he must resume on the morrow, he argued the case with the innkeeper point by point. At dawn he had brought the man back to the Church. This man had been at once so near to, and so far from, the truth, but it took time for the two Castilians to discover the paradox of the religious crisis that flooded this lovely land.

There was scarcely any district in the west of Europe where the life and activities of the Church were more vigorous than in Narbonne. Here, in the time of Charlemagne, the reforming movement among the monks had begun. Here too, in the eleventh century, the reform of the clergy had begun with the Canons Regular at Saint Ruf and had spread to hundreds of chapters in Provence and Spain. The Cistercians, in the twelfth century, had founded here dozens of zealous abbeys. In this district the Church moved forward on a wave of religious fervour, of which in modern times evidence is still to be found in the pure, austere and dignified romanesque style of the church buildings.

At the same time, the Church's protective measures against moral disorder and feudal injustice were stronger here than elsewhere. In the tenth century the bishops of Narbonne had lent their aid to the cause of peace-making, and from this sprang the movement for peace treaties. Unhappily this failed in face of the implacable opposition of the Counts of Toulouse and the Viscounts of Carcassonne who were supported by the King of Aragon. The weeds of anarchy grew quickly in the soil of this factious land. The Church never ceased to renew her appeals for peace and to direct them towards one problem after another: the struggle against the bands of mercenaries, against usury, against the new taxes, against the dangers of the highway. The latest object of the Church's concern was the protection of the Christian Faith, and the slogan "the needs of peace" was changed to "the needs of the Faith and of peace".

The trouble was that the religious enthusiasm of one group of layfolk had taken irregular forms; the feudal lords and the middle class in particular were affected by these errors. From the middle of the twelfth century a large number of heretical preachers, driven out of other parts of Europe, had been gathering in those southern districts where social unrest was preparing the ground for them. Moreover, the merchants and the crusaders had brought back from the East a whole body of new and original speculations. Hence arose the Albigensian sects, to check whom the bishops and the Count of Toulouse were powerless in the last quarter of the century. They had sprung from two completely different sources.

One was the Gospel preaching of the reformers of the eleventh century. The movement for restoring the life of the primitive Church had not only reached the clergy; many capable and enthusiastic laymen, especially in the newly prospering cities, began to follow closely the Gospel teaching and in particular to undertake energetic ventures in proselytism. They chafed at the controls which the traditional authorities of the Church sought to impose, set up their own private communities, and eventually found themselves in open revolt against the Church. Among these were the Vaudois, the followers of Valdes, a converted merchant from Lyons. They surrendered themselves completely to the power of Providence according to the gospel precept, and believed that they were realising the apostolic ideal more perfectly than the clergy when they set out two by two, without gold or silver and their feet shod only in sandals, to preach the kingdom of God. Furthermore, they considered they had the right to exhort one another, to preach, and even offer the sacrifice of the Mass without any authorisation from the Church.

Such also were the Cathari who spread over the South of France with their four bishops, dozens of deacons, thousands of wandering *perfecti* and numerous strict communities. They claimed that they were the authentic successors of the Apostles, and that their primitive hierarchy, their prayers almost entirely confined to the *Pater Noster*, and their sacrament of the *consolamentum*, given in the Holy Spirit the Comforter by the laying on of hands, were all the continuation of the life of the early Church of the martyrs. Their Church, they said, had for long lain hidden in the East; and now that it had come to the West, it was destined to take the place of Rome the usurper, the Babylon of the Apocalypse. Simple folk, who called them The Good Men or The Good Christians, were caught up in admiration for their austerities and detachment from the world, and the overlords, beginning with the new Count Raymond VI of Toulouse, received them with approval. They went about preaching purity, carrying no money with them and dressed in a plain black tunic.

However, on examining their intentions and ideals more carefully, it was disturbing to find that they did not possess that fundamental evangelical virtue of which they took such pains to assume the appearance. The Bogomiles of Bulgaria, from whom they claimed to have received their teachings and their organisation, had revived a religious philosophy that was older than Christ, the dualism of the Gnostics. Ultimately they believed that the spirit of religion and the world they had to live in were absolutely incompatible. One came from a good God, the other from an evil God; so they detested the material world which they said the devil had made, and aimed to cut themselves off from it by means of exaggerated austerities, and through transformation and re-birth to free their holy spirit or the angel imprisoned in their flesh. Hence, sin, sorrow, chastity, salvation did not mean what Our Lord had made them mean. It was no longer true that Christ had saved men by his death and he was not their Lord. The Cross was no longer the source of life but the memory of a defeat. Salvation was not to be gained through a living faith in Jesus Christ, but through freeing oneself from slavery to the created world. Edifying as many of the deeds were to which the knowledge of the gospel spurred them, the fact remains that they rejected Jesus Christ himself. And when we remember the mischief brought about by their contempt for the physical world, and the unbelievable indulgence they showed to the majority of their followers who, unable to imitate the extreme rigorism of the *perfecti*, were promised certain salvation after death, regardless of their present behaviour, because they had received the *consolamentum*, we can imagine the dismay and sorrow of Diego and Dominic embarking on the apostolate in such an equivocal situation.

ENCOUNTER WITH HERESY (1203–1206)

Notes on the four plates that follow:

45 LYONS, THE BIRTHPLACE OF THE VAUDOIS

Here lived Valdes, the rich merchant who was converted in 1173, gave his goods to the poor and set out to preach the Gospel in the same manner as the Apostles. At first he accepted the authority of the bishop as he had promised to do when the Pope authorised him to live according to his ideal (1181), but later he cut himself off from the Church when his enthusiasm for preaching was curbed. The picture shows the church of the ancient abbey of St Martin of Ainay.

46 A CEMETERY OF THE CATHARIST ''PERFECTI''

At Sainte Julienne near Castres.

47 THE CATHARISTS' DOVE OF THE SPIRIT

This dove engraved in copper (about three-quarters of an inch in diameter) was found in the grotto of Ornolac near Ussat (Ariège) to which the Cathari retired. They revered the "good spirit" under this symbol of the Holy Spirit.

48 THE SIGN OF THE FISH

Other traces of the Cathari and their primitive Christian practices have been found in the same grotto. On this rock is the carving of a fish, the symbol of Christ which the early Christians used to paint on the walls of the catacombs.

49 THE FORTIFIED GROTTO OF THE CATHARI AT BOUAN NEAR USSAT

The last of the Cathari, pursued by the Inquisition, withdrew to these limestone caves in the Pyrenees; here they built houses and fortified some of them with perpendicular walls in the rock face.

[24]

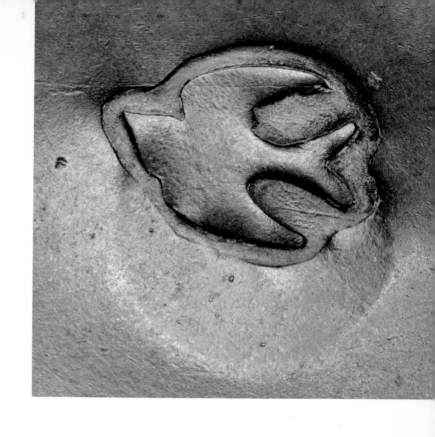

BAREFOOT AND PENNILESS, LIKE THE APOSTLES

JUNE 1206. We are at Montpellier, the Catholic city of Peter of Aragon. Diego and Dominic are again going to meet the Pope in the person of the three Cistercians whom he has commissioned to preach against the heretics. This meeting will be decisive. From this the life of Dominic will take a definite shape. Let us hear the story in the words of Peter of Vaux-Cernai, the chronicler who knew all the participants.

"After leaving the court and reaching Montpellier, Diego met the venerable Arnold, abbot of Cîteaux, and Brother Ralph and Brother Peter of Castelnau, Cistercian monks from Fontfroide who were legates of the Apostolic See. All three had decided to resign from their posts, because so much had been demanded of them that they were discouraged. They had made scarcely any progress in their preaching against the heretics. Whenever they spoke out, the bad lives of the clergy were dragged into the argument in opposition. Yet if they dared to attack clerical slackness, they would be prevented from preaching altogether.

"The bishop's solution to this abortive situation was a simple yet effective scheme. He suggested and even urged that they should take up preaching again with more zeal than ever, should set aside all other cares and should silence wicked tongues by doing their work with humility, match their words with deeds after the example of Our Lord, and go about their job barefoot, without gold or silver, following in every detail the fashion of the Apostles.

"The legates, however, were unwilling to accept this novel advice even from their own superior; they said that, if someone with authority and well enough known was willing to go ahead and put the scheme into operation, they would certainly follow him. What more could be said? Diego, full of the love of God, offered himself. He sent his retinue and his means of transport back to Osma, and himself with one companion only set out from Montpellier with Peter and Ralph, the two legates. The abbot of Cîteaux left for his abbey because shortly there was to be held a general chapter of the Cistercian Order and he wished

[25]

to collect several abbots of his Order to help him carry out his commission of preaching to the heretics more successfully."

The matter is settled. Diego and Dominic (for it is he who is the bishop's companion) give up their work in Osma. They will stay in Narbonne, and undertake the conversion of the Albigenses instead of that of the pagans. The two Cistercians and the two Castilians set out.

The records emphasise the rigour of their daily evangelising. They preach and dispute in public without any ostentation, making no use of their authority but relying solely on the persuasive power of plain truth to give weight to their words. At the same time they put their preaching to the test of sincerity. This was indeed an unusual sight: papal legates, a bishop and a canon "daring to assume contemptible garments in order to speak to despised men, after the example of Christ the poor man": thus, shortly afterwards, the Pope described them in a letter endorsing with his authority their apostolate. Of their belongings they had only retained the books which were necessary for prayer and study. They no longer had any means of their own, and begged their bread from door to door, leaving all in the hands of Providence. They walked barefoot like the Apostles. And also like the Apostles, but unlike the heretics, they had received official commission. "How shall they preach unless they be sent?"

The demeanour of the bishop completely captivated the people. His personal authority swayed the Catholic party from a distance. "Such a moral splendour radiated from the man of God," says one contemporary, "that he gained the affection of the heretics and touched the hearts of all those among whom he lived; moreover, the heretics swore that such a man must be predestined to heaven, and that he must have been sent into their district to learn the true faith."

Following his master and bathed in the splendour of his powerful religious personality, Dominic shared to the full his spirit and his work. The crusading spirit of the Apostles, which he had put into practice at Osma, now blossomed under his eyes. Joyfully he undertook for life the mission to preach and beg his way. Like the others he travelled barefoot. To the end of his days he maintained this custom, but always with the least possible ostentation; he would only take off his shoes when he was out of sight of men and away from the towns. On roads covered with mud, sharp flints or brambles, this was a severe penance. But always he gave himself to it happily because thereby he could to some extent unite himself to the sufferings of Jesus Christ; at the same time he repudiated the excessive literalism of many of the heretics. Remember his cry of joy at the end of a long journey as they were about to engage in disputation, when he saw his own legs and those of the bishop covered in blood: "Beloved," he said, "have high hopes, for the Lord will give us victory. See, our sins are already washed away in blood."

He had just been maliciously misdirected in a dense forest by a friend of the heretics, whom, without the man knowing it, Dominic had deliberately chosen for a guide. The man was totally overcome and converted. At the end of the disputation many others followed his example. The practice of the gospel precepts had opened once again the hearts of the infidels to Christian preaching.

BAREFOOT AND PENNILESS, LIKE THE APOSTLES

Notes on the four plates that follow:

50 THE DISCIPLES AT EMMAUS TRY TO KEEP OUR LORD WHO IS
DRESSED AS A PILGRIM

Bas-relief in the cloister of St Dominic at Silos, a Benedictine house to the north of Caleruega which Dominic often visited. These figures of the Apostles, bearded and barefoot, helped to establish in Dominic's mind the traditional appearance of the Apostles as it was always depicted by mediaeval artists according to the Gospels (Matt. 10:10; Luke 10:4).

51 "HOW BEAUTIFUL ARE THE FEET OF THEM THAT PREACH THE
GOSPEL OF PEACE, OF THEM THAT BRING GLAD TIDINGS OF
GOOD THINGS"

Rom. 10:15. Detail from the preceding bas-relief.

52 DOMINIC WALKING BAREFOOT

"Travelling from place to place Dominic walked barefoot; when he came near his destination he would put his shoes on, but would remove them again after leaving the town . . . and if he happened to hurt his foot on a stone he would smile and say calmly, 'It is a penance'." (*Testimony of Brother John of Spain.*)

53 THE PREACHING OF SAINT PAUL, DOMINIC'S FAVOURITE
APOSTLE

Dominic always carried St Paul's Epistles with him. (*Bas-relief from the abbey of Silos by the sculptor of fig. 50.*)

[28]

THE party of preachers left Montpellier and preached at Servian where the local lord befriended the Catharist bishop. William of Nevers, a French Canon who had apostatised, changed his name to Thierry, and settled in Provence, put up the most vigorous opposition. For a fortnight the argument continued at Béziers, for a week at Carcassonne. They then moved off from Toulouse, only to return to Carcassonne preaching all through Lauragais.

Theological disputations alternated with popular sermons. They used in these disputes the method of debate learned in the schools. The doctrine was set out in formal propositions: the disputants stated their theses in turn and sometimes set them down in writing, naming their authorities in order to give the opponent fair opportunity of stating his own case. At the end of a debate the rival conclusions were summarised in writing and put before arbiters. Juries were also appointed to declare the victors, but they were so often composed of incompetents, feudal lords and ignorant business men, that they shirked the responsibility of reaching a verdict. Dominic had experience of this, and later he told Peter of Vaux-Cernai that a summary he had written was thrown into the fire by the jury to test its truth. The book would not burn, although three attempts were made. Clearly the arbiters found it easier to reach their verdict by a miracle than by reading the evidence.

The people were deeply stirred by the preachers, and sometimes whole villages, declaring themselves for Diego and Dominic, turned out and followed them for miles. But the feudal overlords remained obdurate. The Cathari, after a momentary set-back, resumed the attack most violently, and in March 1207 their bishops and publicity men gathered at Montréal for a full-scale show-down with the Catholics.

DISPUTATIONS WITH THE HERETICS (1206–1207)
Notes on the five plates that follow:

54 SAINT DOMINIC HOLDS A DISPUTATION WITH THE HERETICS
A fresco by Simone Martini in the Spanish chapel of Santa Maria Novella in Florence. Dominic
answers the arguments of his opponents in order, counting off on his fingers. At the bottom
of the fresco black-and-white dogs, representing Dominicans, rescue sheep from wolves who
are devouring them. In the middle ages the dog was the traditional symbol of the preacher:
he barks against error, chases off false shepherds and robbers, and heals with the lick of his
tongue.

55 THE VILLAGE OF CASTELNAU WITH MONTPELLIER IN THE
BACKGROUND
Mendicant preaching started at Montpellier, which thus became the birthplace of the Order
of Preachers.

56 VIEW OF THE CATHEDRAL OF PAMIERS
This picture is taken from the rising ground on which the castle of Raymond-Roger, Count
of Foix, was situated. There, in September 1207, was held the last disputation in which Diego
of Osma took part. It was marked by a fair number of converts, among whom was Arnold of
Crampagna who presided at the disputation and subsequently entered the chapter of the
cathedral, to become sacristan and a life-long friend of Dominic. Among the other converts
was Durand of Huesca and his Vaudois companions, who received permission from the Pope
to continue their apostolic life within the body of the Church under the name of "Poor
Catholics". They became loyal defenders of the faith.

57 SERVIAN, FIRST STOP AFTER LEAVING MONTPELLIER
Perched on a hilltop among cornfields and vineyards, the town was a centre of the Catharist
heresy. After the disputation the enthusiastic populace accompanied the apostolic preachers
for a long way on the road to Béziers, the one shown here in the picture,

IN spite of the length of the disputes, the show-down at Montréal was no more decisive than former ones, but in the end a significant event took place. Arnold, the abbot of Cîteaux and papal legate, had collected thirty monks, including twelve abbots—the same number as the Apostles—to join the preachers. They came barefoot and penniless, following the example of the Apostles down to the last detail, prepared to tackle the heresy with words alone.

Thus the great campaign of preaching which the Pope had appealed for, four years previously, came at last into being. Its official title was "Preaching Christ Jesus", and the people called it "Holy Preaching". The chief director was the abbot of Cîteaux, but the directors of tactics, so to speak, were Diego of Osma and Ralph of Fontfroide. Their authority came direct from the Pope, who had also approved their manner of life and the begging which characterised their itinerant apostolate. Arnold divided the territory between the leading preachers. In each area a headquarters was set up, and in his Diego made arrangements for his men to rest and recover their thoughts and energies between bouts of preaching.

Dominic's district was the border between the dioceses of Carcassonne and Toulouse. This was a hot-bed of Catharism: Fanjeaux, Montréal, Laurac and Mirepoix, all half-way between Carcassonne and Castelnaudary. Dominic settled at Prouille, immediately below Fanjeaux, where the road to Pamiers and the county of Foix leaves the main highway of Lauragais.

The work went on through the spring and early summer with increasing intensity; in August several abbots departed for Bourgogne, where their general chapter was to be held; in September Diego set out for Osma to collect reinforcements. Since the Pope had given formal approval to the mission, he wished to consolidate it with a strong body of preachers who would continue effectually the work begun by the Cistercians. But Diego died at Osma on the 30th of December; Ralph had already died on the 9th of July, and Peter of Castelnau was shortly to be assassinated.

[31]

PREACHING CHRIST JESUS (1207)
Notes on the four plates that follow:

58   THE HAND OF A FRIAR PREACHER

59   THE BOOK THROWN INTO THE FIRE
There are two accounts of this incident, one saying it took place at Fanjeaux, the other at
Montréal; the second version is more probably true, coming from a reliable witness to whom
Dominic himself told the story. The ordeal by fire was by no means uncommon, and was
frequently practised in lay courts where it was believed to reveal God's judgement. (*Bas-relief
by Nicholas Pisano on St Dominic's tomb at Bologna.*)

60   A BEAM PRESERVED IN A CHANTRY OF THE CHURCH AT
FANJEAUX
It is claimed that on this beam can be seen the burns made when Dominic's book leapt out of
the fire three times. At any rate it bears witness to the countless disputations Dominic held
in this little town, where he lived for a long time amidst a large number of feudal families with
Catharist sympathies.

61   NIGHTFALL OVER FANJEAUX OUTLINES THE PLAIN OF
LAURAGAIS
There are two landmarks on the skyline of the town: the church tower (fourteenth century);
and the "Seignadou", a monument marking the scene of a famous event in St Dominic's life.
Looking out over the plain from the top of this rocky height, as he had done in childhood
from the hill above Caleruega, Dominic received a sign from heaven telling him to establish
there the headquarters of his preaching in the dioceses of Toulouse and Carcassonne.

WHILE the missionaries were preaching, Peter of Castelnau, the third papal legate, had bent all his energies to preserving peace and the Christian Faith. This traditional mission, which for so many centuries had bound together the lords spiritual and the lords temporal under the direction of the Pope, had in recent times become much more difficult to pursue because they were now called on not only to maintain peace, to protect the weak and the clergy, to fight usury and additional taxation, and to rid the country of mercenaries, but also to protect the faith of Christian people. If King Peter of Aragon supported the bishops and the legates, the lord of Carcassonne and his feudal followers would attack him; the Count of Toulouse, on the other hand, encouraged the bishops only half-heartedly and on some points opposed them bluntly, especially when it was a question of taxes, mercenaries, or the rights of the clergy which he himself had infringed.

In 1207 Peter of Castelnau succeeded in federating most of the Provençal overlords and the King of Aragon in a peace pact which he made use of to exert pressure on Raymond of Toulouse. So there arose one of those crises in mediaeval Europe when a prince had to choose between the common good of Christendom and his private interests. Brought to bay in this way, Raymond flew into a passion at the legate and threatened to kill him. On the morning of the 14th of January 1208, as he was preparing to cross the Rhône, Peter of Castelnau was assassinated by a member of Raymond's household.

Innocent did not let this crime go unheeded; he took a year to prepare the punishment. The immediate overlord of Raymond was King Philip Augustus, and he was too occupied with his quarrel with England to interfere directly. He therefore allowed an appeal to be made to his vassals, and they gathered at Lyons in great numbers from the Île de France, themselves forming a crusade at the bidding of Arnold in June 1209. Raymond VI, after begging pardon for his own sins, joined the crusade. The whole weight of the army was

[33]

thrown against the Viscount of Carcassonne, young Raymond-Roger Trencavel. The onslaught must have been terrific.

THE CRUSADE IS LAUNCHED (1209)
Notes on the four plates that follow:

62 THE CISTERCIAN ABBEY OF FONTFROIDE NEAR NARBONNE (AUDE)
In answer to the Pope's summons Ralph and Peter of Castelnau set out from here in 1203. On the 26th of January 1205 the Pope wrote a moving letter to encourage Peter, who was longing for the peace of the contemplative life back in his beloved abbey.

63 A FRIGHTENING FIGURE OF A DEVIL BEING EATEN BY A LION
From the façade of St Gilles, the family abbey of the Counts of Toulouse.

64 THE FAÇADE OF THE ABBEY OF SAINT GILLES (GARD)
Twelve and a half miles from Nîmes and not far from the Rhône. It was here that Raymond VI in January 1208 summoned Peter of Castelnau and in a fury threatened him with death. After the murder of Peter some days later, his body was buried in the cloister and eventually transferred to the crypt. Before these steps on the 18th of June 1209, with the crusading armies approaching and to save his lands, Raymond publicly acknowledged his responsibility for the murder, together with a long list of other crimes, in the presence of three archbishops and nineteen bishops. He swore to keep the peace, took the Cross and joined the crusading army.

65 THE BANKS OF THE RHÔNE BETWEEN SAINT GILLES AND ARLES
Near Arles, in the suburb of Trinquetaille, a follower of Raymond who had planted himself in Peter of Castelnau's entourage thrust his lance into the back of the legate on the 14th of January 1208. The crusade began as a result of this murder.

[34]

THE DESTRUCTION OF THE ALBIGENSES

THE Church's forces gathered at Lyons on the 25th of June 1209; in July they were on the march and on the 12th had reached Montélimar. These were soldiers who marched with staves in their hands like the pilgrims to the Holy Land, singing hymns on the way, ready on hearing the call "Au pardon!" to gather and listen to a sermon. But their weapons were following behind with the luggage, and it would be the work of moments to transform this procession into an army of zealots. The North was going to bring the South to heel.

On the 22nd they encamped before Béziers and here met with their first resistance. Raymond-Roger of Béziers-Carcassonne had stirred up the restless townsfolk to defy the crusade, with the result that tents were scarcely pitched before battle was joined; all was so swift that, before the knights could stop them, the rabble in the crusade, had taken control of the situation and, armed with clubs and stones, they seized the city at the first assault. They then began to loot and murder at random, and while the knights attempted in vain to control them, they set the city on fire. It was a most shameful holocaust.

A hundred villages, towns and even castles were evacuated, and the crusading army occupied them without opposition. On the 1st of August they reached Carcassonne; within a fortnight this impregnable fortress had surrendered, and the inhabitants had fled into the country, leaving all their belongings behind. The young Viscount was taken prisoner, and very shortly died in prison; one month later, the whole country was in the hands of the crusaders.

A council of war was held on the field of battle, to discuss putting Béziers-Carcassonne in charge of a crusader who had some connections in the country, and who would eventually become the military leader of the whole campaign. All those who were asked turned it down until eventually Simon de Montfort, the Earl of Leicester, agreed.

THE DESTRUCTION OF THE ALBIGENSES

Notes on the four plates that follow:

66   BÉZIERS ON THE BANKS OF THE ORB (HÉRAULT)
In 1167 the unruly inhabitants of this city killed their lord and wounded their bishop in the church of St Mary Magdalene. In 1205 the bishop was murdered. Nevertheless the city was not given over to Catharism, although it never formally repudiated the few hundred heretics among the population.

67   THE CHURCH OF SAINT MARY MAGDALENE AT BÉZIERS
Seven thousand citizens of all ages took refuge here during the crushing assault which captured the city. They all perished in the tremendous fire started by the attackers. The official records estimate that in the city altogether twenty thousand people lost their lives.

68   THE CITY OF CARCASSONNE COMMANDING THE VALLEY OF THE AUDE
Here can be seen the castle of Raymond-Roger, Viscount of Carcassonne, with its four huge towers and its walls, which still stand to-day as they did in 1209.

69   THE LAMB OF THE APOCALYPSE TRIUMPHANT ON THE CRUSADERS' BANNERS
The lamb, according to Apocalypse 14:1, represents Jesus Christ. The Cross he carries is no longer the sign of his sacrifice but of his victory. The same triumphant lamb appears on the seal of the Preachers of Christ Jesus. It is well known that the Cathari, at least in St Dominic's time, hated the Cross. This is a miniature from a manuscript of the eleventh century, containing the commentary of Beatus de Liébana, in the archives at Osma.

[36]

ATTACKING THE HEIGHTS

Simon de Montfort was the kind of knight who felt little attachment to his own land, and was ready for any enterprise. His faith was staunch, his piety manly and his life blameless; he loved to devote his energies to the cause of the Church, and besides that he was ambitious.

Immediately he took command: he was immensely energetic and daring, always leading the attack on horseback, loyal to his followers, ruthless with enemies and never cast down by set-backs or betrayals. He was at once strategist and tactician. He would always aim at taking the offensive and scattering the enemy either by a thundering charge or by the adroit placing of men and weapons.

He became head of the county on the 15th of August and at once established friendly relations with the local people. Thanks to these folk, a heroic handful who became his loyal followers, he survived the crisis when the first crusaders left him on the completion of their forty day's service. Moreover, he increased his territory so steadily and persistently that the Pope himself grew very concerned about Simon's ambition.

In 1209 he had taken control of the chief cities, Béziers, Carcassonne, Limoux, Albi. During the year 1210, in an epic campaign, he seized, one after another, all the strongholds along the frontiers: Minerve, Termes and Cabaret. These were the last fortresses of the most recalcitrant heretics. In 1211 he turned to the lands of the Count of Toulouse whose relations with the Church were so hostile. In 1212 he turned aside from the siege of the capital itself and occupied the rest of the county with its allies, Comminges and Foix. Finally on the 1st of December he reorganised the whole of the South according to the statutes of Pamiers, after the old French custom. In three and a half years he had thus brought about that unity of the country which had so far eluded the Counts of Toulouse.

This was the task that had been set him: to bring about unity and peace, to safeguard the Church, to abolish "evil customs", remove the mercenaries and drive out the heretics. With regard to this last object, the law of the land, like the law of the Church, expected that active disseminators of heresy should only be exiled, but in the north they had other methods. Frenchmen and Germans conquered by fire, and so did Simon. At Minerve, Termes and Lavaur the crusaders' victory was made sure by huge bonfires into which the Cathari sometimes threw themselves.

ATTACKING THE HEIGHTS
Notes on the four plates that follow:

70   THE STRONGHOLD OF MINERVE (HÉRAULT)
Protected on all sides by deep ravines, it fell on the 22nd of July 1209 after seven weeks of relentless siege in tropical heat. Four catapults and cannon bombarded the walls night and day until they were completely destroyed.

71   LAVAUR ON THE AGOUT
This powerful town of Carcassonne, twenty miles from Toulouse, where many Cathari and knights of the country had taken refuge, was attacked in March 1211. As reinforcements arrived, it was progressively occupied and finally captured on the 3rd of May to the singing of the *Veni Creator*. After the surrender, several hundred *perfecti* were burned in a meadow outside the town.

72   THE FOUR TOWERS OF THE CASTLE OF PETER-ROGER OF CABARET
In an almost unassailable position at Lastours north of Carcassonne, this fortress defied the attacks of the crusaders for a long time. But after a group of its defenders had deserted, it fell to de Montfort in March 1211.

73   THE CASTLE OF QUÉRIBUS, THE LAST STRONGHOLD OF THE CATHARI
This castle only fell in 1255, long after the end of the Albigensian war.

[38]

By 1213 Simon was master of the greater part of the county of Toulouse, except for Montauban and the capital town which, like the Count himself, was excommunicated. But from Spain long-expected reinforcements were coming from Peter of Aragon, who had gained prestige in the greatest of the victories over Islam, at Las Navas de Tolosa. Realising that he was threatened by the whole of southern France, he went to Rome and negotiated on the spot. But finding he could get no satisfaction from the Pope, he threw in his lot against the crusade and the Church and marched on Toulouse.

The decisive battle was fought on the 12th of September. On the plain of Muret, de Montfort charged an army twice as large as his own with such fury that he shattered them and drove them back to the Garonne. The King of Aragon was killed, and Raymond VI and his son took refuge in the court of the King of England. Simon entered Toulouse, and the county and the whole of Provence passed into his hands. In January 1215, the whole Church of the region petitioned the Pope to name Simon "prince et monarque", independent even of Philip. This meant establishing a kingdom larger than that of France, and would have been a sure remedy for the anarchy in the district, had it not been founded on the dispossession of all the local overlords to the advantage of the crusaders from the north.

After a few months, Innocent III resumed the position of arbiter, and in November 1215 he named Simon Count of Toulouse, but appointed the son of Raymond VI to the Marquisate of Provence. This was a fateful nomination, for when in June 1216 Simon returned from a victorious journey where Philip had received him with honour, he found Raymond VII installed at Beaucaire, and for the first time in his life he was unable to dislodge his enemy. One after another, rebellions flared up. In vain Simon repeated his audacious tactics of earlier years, daring charges, lightning raids from the Alps to the Pyrenees. Toulouse was seething with revolt, and at the end of 1217 it broke out. There was a long siege in which Simon's skill and courage seemed powerless; his best friends were killed, his own energies were consumed by ten long years of unceasing warfare and his enthusiasm was damped by set-backs. Fighting alone now, his great courage sustained him in what he believed was the cause of God. And then, on the 25th of June 1218, a weapon "which a woman could use" shot the missile "as straight as could be". He fell, "dead, bleeding and black".

RISE AND FALL OF DE MONTFORT (1213–1218)
    Notes on the eight plates that follow:

74   SEAL OF SIMON DE MONTFORT (*Archives nationales, Paris*)

75   THE GARONNE BETWEEN TOULOUSE AND MURET
     The river, which divides the two districts, was a great obstacle to the Toulousains and Aragonais in their flight, and made their defeat all the more serious.

76   THE BATTLEFIELD OF MURET
     This field lies to the south of the district where Simon had come to help the garrison. A river and a stream both crossed the battlefield at the end occupied by the southern armies and hampered their manœuvres. Simon made up for being outnumbered by the vigour of his attacks. Muret was the only battle in the Albigensian war to be fought in open country.

77   SEAL OF PETER OF ARAGON (*Archivo historico nacional, Madrid*)

78
79   KNIGHTS CHARGING
     Painted wooden strips from a thirteenth-century ceiling, preserved in the museum at Narbonne.

80   THE "STONE OF THE SIEGE" (*Bas-relief in the cathedral of Carcassonne.*)
     A representation of the siege of Toulouse in which Simon de Montfort lost his life. All the details are contemporary. To the left are the attackers wearing square helmets, then a slope where they struggle; in the middle is a wall defended by knights armed with lance and shield and wearing pointed helmets on which can be seen the seal of Peter of Aragon (fig. 77). At the top to the right is a cross-bowman on a tower, and higher still angels are carrying the souls of the dead from the town, which shows that the sculptor was on the side of the besieged. In the bottom right-hand corner is a stone-throwing catapult with six men pulling the ropes and others supplying the stones.

81   TOMB OF AN UNKNOWN CRUSADER AT FONTFROIDE

THE FIRST FOUNDATION AT PROUILLE (1207–1213)

While the bloodshed was spreading over the South, Dominic continued to preach alone. Sadly alone, for Ralph was dead, most of the Cistercian abbots had returned to France, Peter of Castelnau had been murdered and, worst of all, Diego had departed for good. But Dominic was not alone in his prayers, for Diego, in addition to inspiring and leading Dominic in his mendicant preaching had, before departing, founded a small community of nuns at Prouille.

This community consisted of young women who had broken away from the Cathari after being entrusted to them in their youth (as was the custom in the South among impoverished noble families), of women converts from Catharism and the Vaudois, and of well-born ladies of Catholic birth.

The evangelical sects, and Catharism in particular, at this time made a strong appeal to female generosity. The absolute chastity of the *perfecti*, their detachment from everything worldly and material, and their extreme spirituality, appealed to the women's purity, generosity and absolute goodness. So the heretics recruited not only more *perfecti*, but some of their most effective propagandists. The *perfecti* lived in communities which eventually became both rest houses and centres of study for their preachers, and also institutions for the care and education of any children whom they might introduce.

In proportion as the disputations with the papal missionaries increased, the importance of converts from among women grew. The problem became crucial, because these women found themselves penniless, disowned by their families who adhered to Catharism, and did not know what to do with themselves. Diego believed that they ought to be able to find in the Church a way of life at once more holy and more fruitful than that which they had led outside. He therefore decided to found a convent with these convert women and others who were already seeking to enter religion. In fact, Dominic had brought about most of these conversions, so he undertook to approach the Count and ask his assistance. The archbishop of Narbonne gave them an endowment to start with in April 1207, and a community was founded at Prouille which Dominic made his base of operations. There he found all the spiritual life and strength which Diego had instilled into the community before his departure.

God had given Dominic a special grace for helping women: wherever he went, Fanjeaux, Toulouse, Madrid, Rome, Bologna, he would leave a community of women together with a larger number of men's monasteries. It is appropriate that his first foundation should have been for women. His deep sensitive chastity gave his devotion to them a chivalrous character which increased his freedom and power. On their side, their generosity and spiritual enthusiasm sustained his high spirits. And in addition, the economic security of a community of women who were able to accept gifts counterbalanced the mendicant life of the preachers. On returning from a spell of preaching during which he had begged his bread on the road from day to day, Dominic could enjoy the hospitality of the Sisters just as the Catharist preachers enjoyed that of the *perfecti*. But most important, their prayers were added to his. The splendour of his preaching and his life found its source in the religious splendour of this community, and whenever anyone wanted to give a donation to the convent, they always said they were offering it for the "Holy Preaching" of Master Dominic.

From 1207 to the middle of 1209, Dominic's life was divided between staying at the convent and making preaching tours: leaving Prouille as a kind of headquarters, he would range through Castelnaudary, Pamiers and Carcassonne. Then the crusade was launched; Simon settled in the castle at Fanjeaux, and Dominic got to know him. At the same time Foulques, the Cistercian bishop of Toulouse, took advantage of the temporary goodwill of Raymond VI and the citizens to engage Dominic to preach in the capital. This continued throughout 1210 and into 1211; Dominic only returned to Prouille for brief stays. On each visit he observed a growing problem: the community was gradually increasing but their income remained static.

On the 12th of April 1211 Toulouse was excommunicated and the preachers left. Foulques and de Montfort then made their first gift to the convent at the request of Dominic. From now on, all his attention was given to the convent.

To begin with, they must be satisfactorily endowed. Several friends in the district gave donations; then some of the crusaders, whom de Montfort had installed in the confiscated lands, followed suit. Dominic contrived by selling and exchange to increase the value of these gifts. So by 1212–1213 he was well on the way to erecting a suitable building, and everyone was talking about "the new convent".

At this time also he proceeded to settle the rule and enclosure of the convent. There was set up a home of prayer and holiness, which still flourishes in the twentieth century.

THE FIRST FOUNDATION AT PROUILLE (1207–1213)

Notes on the five plates that follow:

82 PROUILLE SEEN FROM THE "SEIGNADOU" OF FANJEAUX

The abbey is in the middle of the picture. The winding road which Dominic often took
between Prouille and Fanjeaux can be seen starting at the bottom edge of the picture.

83 CHARTERS RECORDING THE GIFTS OF SIMON DE MONTFORT
    TO PROUILLE

Reading from the bottom upwards: the very first benefaction of May 15th 1211; then those
of August 5th and December 1st 1212. (*Archives de l'Aude, Carcassonne.*)

84 SEAL OF THE SISTERS' CONVENT AT PROUILLE

(*Archives nationales, Paris.*)

85 CHARTERS OF SALE AND GIFT AT PROUILLE

Reading from the bottom upwards: two sales for the purpose of enlarging the grounds of the
convent in May 1213; a gift from a Frenchman, October 16th 1212; a gift from a citizen of
Prouille, December 22nd 1215; the gift of a hostel at Toulouse from Bishop Foulques, 1215.
(*Archives de l'Aude, Carcassonne.*)

86 THE LAND OF THE TAICH

This was part of the original endowment from the archbishop of Narbonne, as was the church
of St Martin of Limoux which can be seen at the extreme right of the picture.

[44]

...com̄ lc̄ic̄ duc̄ monꝰ factꝰ dr̄ p̄missione b̄ic̄ ꞇ karꝰ uicecom̄. uniūsir p̄ntcꝰ
lr̄as inspecturis salt. Houir uniūsitas ūa q̄d nos assensu .d. dilecte uxo
ris n̄re ꞇ .d. p̄mogenitꝰ nr̄i p̄ remediū anime n̄re ꞇ anccessoꝝ nr̄oꝝ
dedim̄ in elemosinā deo ꞇ ecc̄tie b̄e marie de p̄uillano ꞇ ibidem q̄ uisanti
bus duos campos tr̄e q̄ fuerūt dn̄e ecc̄tie. unū ap̄d montē Baio ꞇ aliū
ap̄d Bezant̄ quos uolum̄. innuari ꞇ tr̄a que erat iuxta ecc̄tiam que clau
dir cū eadem ecc̄tia ad ampliendas ensdem dom̄ officinas. Insuꝑ dedim̄ mē
brom ꞇ uillam p̄ntam indecimario de Sauzeur ad usū. ꞇ aratro̜ bouum
.i.x̄. arpenta uineaꝝ in eodem decimario cū ingressib̄ ꞇ egressib̄ suis ꞇ aq̄s
ꞇ pasturis suis. p̄terea eciam dedim̄ p̄dicte ecc̄tie tr̄am ad usū .ii. aratro
rū de hereditate q̄ uillari ꞇ fr̄es sui ap̄d uillariū possidebant. ꞇ unam
uineam ꞇ ortū ibidm̄ ꞇ inibi uim̄ ibidm̄ capellanū p̄ anima gaut̄r̄d de
Healsha ad usum cu̅s dedim̄. iii. mod t̄ frumenti sepedicte ecc̄tie. annuatim
ap̄d uillariū ꞇ lauzed capiendos. p̄ea dedim̄ p̄dicte ecc̄tie .xuii. den tol ꞇ
dn̄ia q̄ ipsi p̄tinent q̄s Ar. karndr debebat facē oiabile ꞇ uxro suo ber
ardo. hec oia dedim̄ p̄dicte ecc̄tie libe ꞇ q̄ete ꞇ p̄petuo possidenda. Quod
ut ratū ꞇ in cōcussū habeat ōi tempore p̄ntem paginam sigilli nr̄i muni
mine fecim̄ roboꝛari. Data ap̄d ap̄nnia̅. Anno dn̄i .ō̄. cc̄. xii. kl̄. decemb̄

1213. DOMINIC, still young and unburdened with responsibility, gave himself whole-heartedly to the care of souls. Those who met him in these days never forgot that apostolic face: hardy, warm-hearted, ascetic and full of love.

"He devoted himself to the work with such enthusiasm," says William Peyre, the abbot of the chapter of Narbonne, "that he would have liked to preach the word of God day and night, in church, in private houses, in the fields and on the roads, always to the point and speaking of nothing but God. He gave no quarter to the heretics, and attacked them with sermons, public disputations and every means in his power"; "as much by words," adds Arnold of Crampagna, "as by the example of a holy life."

"He never allowed himself to be discouraged by persecution. He was always cool and collected in the midst of dangers, and never allowed himself to be turned aside by fear. Whenever he found himself overcome by sleep, there and then he would lie down by the road or on ground near by and fall asleep." Blessed Otho adds: "One day, while he was travelling with some companions and myself through the woods, he lagged behind. When we went to look for him, we found him on his knees in prayer, without any thought for the wolves who often attacked large crowds of people."

"One day," says Peter de Brunet, "the holy man had crossed a river by boat, and the ferrymen demanded a penny fare. Dominic had no money, but they insisted, demanding either a penny or a pledge, and they seized hold of him. He turned his eyes to the ground and pointing to a penny there, he said, 'Take what you want from the ground.'"

"He was often afflicted with great pains," said Guillelma with whom he used to stay. "Those who happened to be near on these occasions would put him to bed, but I often saw him get up quickly and lie on the ground, for he was not in the habit of resting on a bed." "Very often," adds Bécède, "I prepared the bed for him, but he never used it; in the morning I would find it exactly as I had left it after making it the previous evening. The same thing happened when he was ill; very often I would find him stretched on the ground without any blankets; I would cover him up, but if I came back later I would always find him saying his prayers, either standing up or prostrate. When he had a meal with me—which he did more than two hundred times—he ate little more than a couple of eggs, though I would set several dishes before him."

"I never saw anyone," says William Peyre, "who prayed so much or wept so copiously. When he was at prayer, he would cry so loudly that everyone in the neighbourhood could hear him, and he would say through his tears, 'Lord, have mercy on your people. What will become of sinners?' He would spend whole nights on his kness, weeping and bemoaning the sins of others."

BROTHER DOMINIC, PREACHER
Notes on the four plates that follow:

87 THE AMBUSH ON THE ROAD TO FANJEAUX
In the foreground can be seen the corner where ruffians waited to seize Dominic alive and hand him over to the mercy of his cruel enemies. A cross, called the assassin's cross (seen here from the side), marks the traditional spot of the ambush.

88 SECTION OF THE ANCIENT WALLS OF FANJEAUX
Dominic passed between these two walls on the way up to Prouille to minister to the town which was largely given over to heresy.

89 SAINT DOMINIC'S HOUSE AT FANJEAUX
This house is held in veneration because St Dominic lived there, perhaps from 1211, at least in 1214. The fireplace is modern but the little oven ancient. It is reasonably certain that this room was behind the church where the ancient saddle-room of the castle would have been situated. It is a setting to stir the imagination. A Dominican lay-brother is making the fire.

90 SAINT DOMINIC'S FOUNTAIN NEAR MONTRÉAL
When he came to a place, Dominic would quench his thirst at a wayside fountain so as not to embarrass his host. Traditionally this particular spring is associated with this habit of his, because it lies half-way along the road from Prouille to Carcassonne which Dominic so often travelled.

[46]

AT THE SERVICE OF THE BISHOPS (1213–1214)

BETWEEN 1211 and 1213 the chief dioceses of Narbonne were re-established. The new bishops were chosen from among the Preachers of Christ Jesus. Arnold of Cîteaux became archbishop of Narbonne, and Guy of Vaux-Cernai, the last one remaining of the twelve abbots who came from de Montfort's country and who was a friend of his, became bishop of Carcassonne. But Dominic twice declined a bishopric for which he had several times been nominated. He preferred to preach from the vantage-point of humility, not that of authority.

He did not preach, however, without authorisation. Although he had only recently been authorised by the papal legates, he now received another mandate from the bishop of Carcassonne. In the spring of 1213, Guy, who was returning to France for a while, named Dominic his vicar *in spiritualibus*. Dominic settled at Bishop's House among the spires of the city and preached the whole of Lent. These were disturbed days: the irresolution of Raymond VII, Peter II, and even Pope Innocent III himself, supporting now one, now another of the warring parties, made everyone very unsettled. But Dominic never allowed this to hold up his work; he reckoned that it was his business always to preach and to "set aside all other cares".

On the return of Guy he went back to Prouille. Now it was the turn of Bishop Foulques to find him work, and he put him in charge of Fanjeaux. Dominic took the winding road that climbs out of Prouille, settled in the district and set to work methodically where he had already often worked in short spells. The knights who lived there were friends of the Cathari. They threatened him, but death had no terrors for him, and pains of martyrdom, such as those which the Count of Foix inflicted on the crusaders and priests he held prisoner, were in Dominic's eyes a privilege from the Lord. They would only be the crown of the continual offering of himself that he was making through his labours and penances for the conversion of sinners.

Little by little, companions joined him in his preaching. He had a house and a small income provided by the bishop, and the Count had added a stipend. They were planning to establish at Fanjeaux a community of men who would go about the diocese in evangelical poverty, preaching the word of God and always accessible. Once again the Preaching of Christ Jesus had come to life, Diego's magnificent plan had been realised.

AT THE SERVICE OF THE BISHOPS (1213–1214)
Notes on the five plates that follow:

91 THE ROMANESQUE CHURCH WHERE DOMINIC PREACHED THROUGHOUT LENT, 1213
The cathedral of St-Nazaire at Carcassonne.

92 THE SQUARE TOWER OF THE BISHOP'S PALACE
This tower dates from after the beginning of the thirteenth century, but it is found on the site of the episcopal palace at Carcassonne where Dominic lived.

93 THE PROUD CITY OF CARCASSONNE
Although the fortifications were strengthened during the Middle Ages, and the towers have had slate roofs added in the time of Viollet-le-Duc in the nineteenth century, the general lay-out is the same as in Dominic's time.

94 THE FIELD OF THE STORM
"Brother Bertrand told me that during a journey he made with Master Dominic a great storm arose. Torrential rain had already soaked the ground, but by simply making the sign of the cross the Saint stopped the downpour so close in front of him that, as they both walked forward, they could see the rain pouring down only three paces ahead, and not a single drop even touched the hem of their clothes." This incident, related by Jordan of Saxony, is traditionally believed to have taken place on the spot shown in this picture near to Montréal. Bartholomew of Trent, however, a contemporary of Dominic, puts it on the road to Rome.

95 A PENNY OF THE COUNT OF TOULOUSE
This recalls the episode of the boatman told in a previous section. (*Musée Dupuis, Toulouse.*)

THIS work began again, not actually at Fanjeaux, but at Toulouse on the request of the papal legate who had just been presiding at the Council of Montpellier. But now the preaching was not to be done in casual groups as it had been previously; Dominic's experience had taught him that such schemes were not sufficiently cogent. A permanent preaching programme was needed, capable of supporting itself and providing its own replacements. In other words, some sort of religious order was necessary. In this way, if a regular community were established, continuity of work would be assured and a steady increase of men and materials, as well as a religious headquarters to provide the intellectual and moral training the preacher so urgently needed.

Two influential merchants from Toulouse came to Dominic's assistance. One of them, Peter Seila, gave him a group of houses next door to a château belonging to the Church. So the foundation was ready and became a reality between the 7th and 25th of April 1215 when Dominic received the vows of the first brethren. Dominic was now a founder, and the houses of Peter Seila near the gate of Toulouse were the cradle of the Dominican Order. At the beginning of June 1215 Bishop Foulques of Toulouse signed a Charter approving the "regular life" of the new community and formally appointing each of its members a preacher in his diocese.

In the name of Our Lord Jesus Christ We bring to the notice of everyone now and in the future that we Foulques, by the grace of God humble minister in the see of Toulouse, in order to uproot heresy, destroy vice, teach the Creed and instil the moral law, appoint as preachers in our diocese Brother Dominic and his companions, whose rule of life is to live in religious community and travel on foot preaching the word of God in evangelical poverty.

But since the labourer is worthy of his hire, since one should not muzzle the ox which treads the thrashing floor and most of all because they who preach the Gospel should live by the Gospel, we wish that these men, so long as they go abroad preaching, should receive their sustenance and everything necessary from the diocese. With the consent of the chapter of the church of Blessed Stephen and of the clergy of the diocese, we dedicate in perpetuity to the said preachers and to all who, moved by the love of God and zeal for souls, prepare themselves for this same work of preaching in the same way, a half of that third part of the tithe which is devoted to the furnishings and fabric of all the parish churches which are in our charge, so that they can clothe themselves, obtain what they need when they are sick, and rest when they require. Whatever moneys are left over at the end of the year we lay down that they shall be returned for the use of the aforesaid churches or for the poor as the bishop shall see fit. Since the law provides that a part of the tithes shall be devoted to the poor, it seems clear that we should assign a part of those moneys to those who have embraced evangelical poverty for Christ.

Given in the year of the Incarnation 1215, in the reign of Philip King of the French, Count de Montfort holding the principality of Toulouse and Foulques being bishop.

The regular programme of the brothers was not as simple as might appear. There were two sides to the life. One half consisted of itinerant preaching: this was the life which Dominic, following closely the example of the Apostles, had pursued for nine years and was to continue till his death. Here was true mendicant preaching with every detail fixed by custom. But now, in addition, there was the regular life in community where the brothers formed their characters, studied, rested, and when they were ill came for cure. Their maintenance was guaranteed by the allowance the bishop made them from diocesan funds, but a number of restrictions were to make this source of income precarious.

The fact was that the attempt in the Charter of 1215 to combine two kinds of poverty was unsatisfactory. Living on diocesan funds, while they were preparing their work or resting at the convent, was certainly living on alms given to Christ's poor according to tradition. But accepting this regular income conflicted with the daily abandonment to Divine Providence which had been the original ideal of the preacher. In 1215 Dominic and his companions could not see how to combine the two.

A preaching mandate from a bishop was a new thing. Until now the preachers had received their authorisation "against the heretics" from the Pope. This had been defensive preaching or, at best, preaching to make converts. Dominic and his brothers were now widening their scope; the object of their work was the same as the object of a bishop in his widest pastoral mission. This meant positive preaching of doctrine and Christian morals to the whole diocese, faithful and otherwise. From now on, the Dominican preacher co-operates with the bishop from whom exclusively he receives his authority for his pastoral mission. The Preachers of Toulouse—this was the name given to the brethren in these early years—became a permanent instrument for evangelising the diocese.

PREACHING IN TOULOUSE (1215)

Notes on the four plates that follow:

96 THE HOUSE OF PETER SEILA, CRADLE OF THE DOMINICAN
ORDER

This "house with stone floors" (Jordan), which in the thirteenth century lay close to the walls
of Toulouse, still exists: it is the building to the left of the single-storied house. The triangular
pediment of the door is more modern. In 1920 the old room in which St Dominic slept near
the first brethren was still the chapel, but unfortunately it has now gone and the room is let
to a tenant.

97 THE APSE AND THE MAGNIFICENT TOWER OF THE ABBEY
CHURCH OF SAINT SERNIN AT TOULOUSE

In the time of St Dominic the abbey became the permanent home of the chapter of Toulouse.
It was famous for its relics of the Apostles.

98 AN OLD MAP OF TOULOUSE (1631)

The oval outline of the old French-romanesque walls with several additions can be seen;
these were in existence in St Dominic's time. The house of Peter Seila (No 38 on the plan)
lies by the Narbonne gate in front of the castle of Narbonne, the earl's castle. The gate of
St Michael (A on the plan) occupies the site of the castle, fifteen yards from the river. The
church of St Romain (No 43 on the plan), of which there will be more to say later, lies just
above the inscription *r. de St Rome* at the western end of the straight main road that runs
across the town (upper left centre in the plan).

99 AN EVANGELIST

Romanesque carving from the crypt of Saint Sernin.

THE POPE APPROVES (1215, 1217)

FROM all parts of Europe bishops were converging on Rome for the Fourth General Council of the Lateran. Foulques set out with all the dignitaries of Narbonne, and Dominic was in their company.

The records make it quite plain that Dominic and his bishop were going to ask the Pope to confirm and add the weight of papal sanction to some of Foulques' ordinances, thus rendering them permanent. They wished him to confirm from the start the revenues dedicated to the convent by the Count and the bishop, but chiefly they wanted him to grant them the right both to call themselves and to be an order of preachers.

This was a delicate matter. Of all the problems that beset and disturbed the Church in this century, preaching was one of the greatest. Bishops certainly had neither the time nor the energy nor, in some cases, had they the knowledge for preaching, and in some of the dioceses which were very extensive they were just not equal to the task of breaking the word of God to the faithful. And this was the cause of heresies. The tenth canon of the Lateran Council states this in clear terms, and commands bishops to set up in their dioceses groups of exemplary preachers who will do this work for them. But it was another matter to entrust this work blindly to all the members of a community such as Foulques had just set up, so that a man would have a mandate for preaching by the simple fact that he belonged to that community. This was an entirely new idea, and only the Pope himself could approve it.

And if the members of this community were going to practise evangelical poverty, there was even greater cause for concern. The bishops knew from bitter experience—and here in Rome they could easily press the point—that the most serious disorders among their flocks had been brought about by those bands of apostolic preachers who were likely to crop up anywhere. On this point the bishops would be unanimous: no more wandering missionaries, no new ways of religious life. The thirteenth canon of the Council was firm on the point. The Pope alone could confirm Dominic's way of life that Foulques had already ratified.

The Pope was favourable. He asked the bishop to provide a church in his diocese for the Dominican preachers as evidence that they were incorporated into the diocesan clergy. He told Dominic and his brethren to choose a rule already approved so as to establish themselves within a guaranteed tradition, and then to return to Rome. He promised in advance that if this was done he would give them on the spot the three approvals they desired: of the revenues, the title and the work of preaching.

THE POPE APPROVES (1215, 1217)

Notes on the four plates that follow:

100 MOSAIC OF THE APOSTLES IN THE OLD LATERAN PALACE

This mosaic adorns the aspe at the end of the great hall, the only remnant of the papal palace where, in November 1215, the chief discussions of the fourth Council took place.

101 THE APOSTLES PETER AND PAUL APPEAR TO SAINT DOMINIC WHILE HE IS AT PRAYER IN SAINT PETER'S

Paul gives him a book signifying the power to teach, and Peter a staff signifying authority. The chronicler who tells this story adds that Dominic then saw the brethren going two by two to preach all over the world. This vision (?1217) paved the way for the spread of the Order. (*Bas-relief by Nicholas Pisano on the tomb of St Dominic at Bologna.*)

102 POPE INNOCENT III DREAMS THAT DOMINIC HOLDS UP THE LATERAN PALACE

The story of this vision spread throughout the Order from 1247 onwards; it was not, however, a vision of St Dominic but of St Francis whose name had been omitted. But it does represent the true feelings of the Popes towards Dominic as expressed, for instance, in the bull of Canonisation. (*Bas-relief by Nicholas Pisano on the tomb at Bologna.*)

103 POPE HONORIUS III GIVES DOMINIC THE PROMISED CONFIRMATIONS

Although Nicolas Pisano here represents the confirmation of a book, it was only particular points of law which were confirmed. The Dominican constitutions were never presented to the Pope for confirmation in their entirety.

[54]

FOULQUES gave Dominic not one but three churches, so that he could settle in each of them a community of preaching brothers. One was at Toulouse, the church of St Romain; another was near Pamiers on the road to Foix; and the third was near Puylaurens going towards Albi. As Dominic had had the church at Fanjeaux on the road to Carcassonne since 1214, this meant that a network of preachers was now spread right over the diocese of Toulouse. Not only the diocese was touched but the whole of the Albigensian territory, however little other bishops might welcome the preachers in their own dioceses. Already Arnold the legate had divided the territory among the Preachers of Christ Jesus; Dominic's network was securely established in another fashion.

The brethren gathered at Toulouse in their make-shift convent to choose a recognised religious rule. They chose the Rule of St Augustine, and thus entered the category of Clerks Regular. After the manner of Dominic himself, their life combined that of a Canon and that of an evangelical preacher. The two apostolic ideals of prayer in private and preaching in the market square were both present. These two aspects of the life of the twelve Apostles were linked in the same way that the two forms of poverty were. From 1215 onwards these ways of life began to combine and at the same time the observance of the precepts of St Augustine's rule hardly altered the fashion of their community life.

But to the fundamental precepts must be added religious customs and observances without which it is impossible to organise daily life in the monastery or to train novices. So Dominic and his brethren developed a number of customs concerning liturgy, fasting, sleep, wearing wool, and chapter of faults, which they copied from the Canons of the strict observance at Prémontré. Thus Dominican law-making began. The Order which now bears the title "Order of Preachers" was between 1216 and 1218 springing into life.

Dominic went to Rome. Pope Innocent III was dead, but Ugolino, the most influential of the Cardinals, had pledged his friendship to Dominic, for he wished to work with him for the salvation of souls. He spoke for him to the new Pope, Honorius III. On the 22nd of December 1216 and the 21st of January 1217 Dominic received from Honorius the confirmations promised by his predecessor, together with the title "Order of Preachers" for his followers.

SAINT ROMAIN

Notes on the four plates that follow:

104 THE PRIVILEGE OF CONFIRMATION

The *Rota* with the Pope's signature and those of eighteen Cardinals given in the course of a Consistory. This parchment brought back by Dominic to Saint Romain in the winter of 1217 passed from the archives of the convent at Toulouse to those of Haute-Garonne where it is to be found to-day.

105 A CHASUBLE SAID TO BE SAINT DOMINIC'S

This precious chasuble of the twelfth century is kept among the treasures at Saint Sernin in Toulouse, and is traditionally believed to have belonged to St Dominic. This does not at all accord with his emphatic pronouncements about poverty.

106 COMMUNION OF THE BRETHREN AT SAINT ROMAIN

At the beginning of 1217 there were scarcely fifteen in the community. The priory was small, but the brothers had cells, or at least cubicles in a dormitory which were "adequate for study and sleep". This picture shows the young preachers of the priory of Saint Maximin.

107 DOMINIC PERFORMS A MIRACLE: THE PILGRIMS SAVED FROM DROWNING

This incident, which occurred during a siege of Toulouse, may have taken place in 1217 or perhaps in 1211. Some English pilgrims to Compostella found themselves sinking in the Garonne with the boat that was carrying them, when Dominic's prayer brought them to the surface long enough to be saved. (*Painting of Borassa in the diocesan museum at Vich near Barcelona.*)

[56]

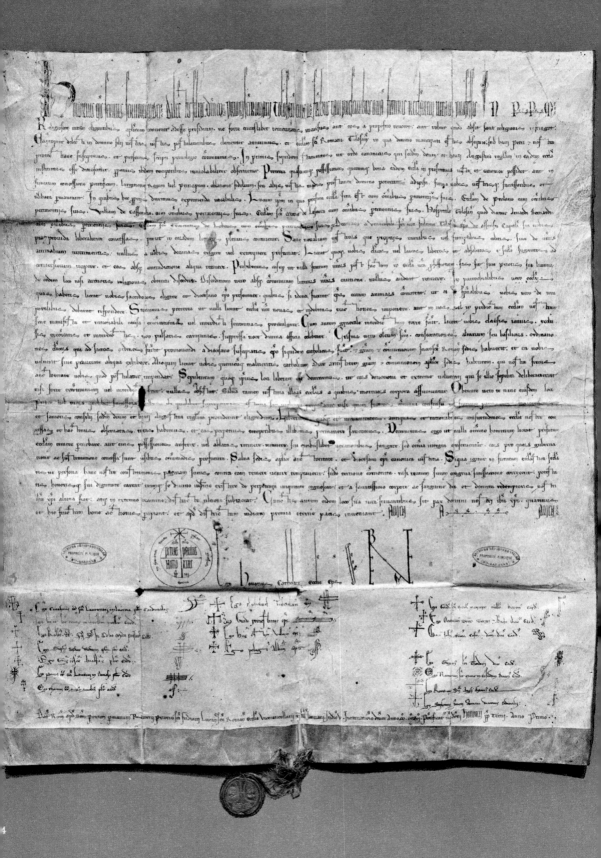

DOMINIC AT PRAYER

COMPLINE is finished, and the brethren have said their private prayers and gone to bed. Dominic thinks he is now alone and begins to pray aloud and groan and mortify his body. He is unaware of one of the brethren concealed behind a pillar, watching him in the dim light of the sanctuary. More than one of the brethren did this, and we have to thank their curiosity for our knowledge of Dominic's prayer. This prayer, which went on for hours, was the secret mystery at the heart of Dominic's work.

He always prayed: during office, at Mass, on the road, in the woods, wherever they visited on their journeys. Especially at night did he pray. The moment they arrived at their lodging, soaked with rain, Dominic began to pray while the others would be drying themselves before the fire. He often spent the whole night in this fashion, only breaking his private prayer to go to Matins, where he would spur on the others to sing louder, or to go to the dormitory and cast a loving eye over the sleeping brethren, and cover them up again if the bedclothes were slipping off. He himself had no bed. He would sleep in the church between his prayers, with the altar step for a pillow. They would also find him curled up in this same fashion in some corner of the convent, or lying on a bench, or asleep sitting up. He often fell asleep at meals, and would sometimes on a journey lie down to sleep on the roadside. He gave his days to men and his nights to God.

His prayer was so intense that he ceased to be aware of his surroundings, and his body mirroring the movements of his soul would be agitated, and he would bend down, prostrate himself perhaps in tears, or he would be caught up in a rapture of happiness. Between whiles he disciplined his body most harshly. Even during sickness he disciplined himself so, and at the height of the fever the movements of his lips and the look on his face indicated the intensity of his spiritual life. Some people saw him on these occasions so carried out of himself by spiritual power that he seemed to have left this world altogether.

It was always Jesus Our Saviour he spoke to, before the altar or the crucifix which he loved to visit. He prayed in reparation for wrongs, he prayed for the suffering, for sinners or for his brethren. Each emotion in turn was reflected in his mobile face. Sometimes sadness of spirit made him cry out, but always in the end he found peace and radiant joy.

This all-embracing prayer was behind the discernment and courage of his preaching, and the assurance of his decisions of policy. It was during such a prayer-vision in St Peter's in Rome that he decided to withdraw the brethren completely from their original work against the Albigenses, and to send them out in pairs across the whole world.

DOMINIC AT PRAYER

Notes on the ten plates that follow:

Fresco by Fra Angelico in a novice's cell in the priory of San Marco, Florence.

DOMINIC'S NINE WAYS OF PRAYING

The following miniatures are illustrations from the Codex Rossianus No. 3 in the Vatican Library, a little work from the last quarter of the thirteenth century, which gathers together the stories told by St Dominic's contemporaries about his behaviour during prayer.

WHEN Dominic brought back from Rome the papal approval, the brethren were overjoyed and the whole convent was *en fête*. A hostel near the Arnold-Bernard gate had been given to Dominic, and it was now occupied by a group of young women who had left a life of sin to take up the religious life. The Pope had confirmed the foundation at Prouille, and the convent was flourishing; a group of the brethren ministered to the community, and also to the parish at Fanjeaux. They were all filled with hope and cheerfulness in their work for God and for souls.

Dominic, however, knew that this would not last for long. The first murmurings of rebellion against the northern crusaders were to be heard in Toulouse and throughout the country. De Montfort was suffering one set-back after another at the hands of Raymond VII, and only kept a grip on Toulouse by means of brutalities which were destroying his good name among the people. If war should break out again, it would be more barbarous than ever and there would no longer be room for preaching. It was among the faithful themselves that there would be most need for eloquence.

The time had come for decisive action, and it seems that Dominic chose Whit Sunday, the 14th of May 1217, as the time, and St Romain as the place, for his decision. "He prayed to the Holy Spirit, and called the brethren together and told them that he had decided, in spite of their small numbers, to send them out to preach all over the world; the scattering was to be so complete that from now on they should never live together again."

This was a heavy blow for the brethren, and even the most courageous were daunted. They were well aware of their limitations: most of them were young, imperfectly instructed, and scarcely fully acquainted with their new form of life, and already they must cut loose from their roots and go out to preach. In later years, several of them recalled their terror at going out into the unknown, made harder by parting from one another. The majority of them trusted Dominic's wisdom and the power of the prayers he had promised, but there

[59]

was at least one who rebelled.

The friends of St Romain were flabbergasted. De Montfort, Foulques and Arnold of Narbonne felt they had been let down, and they were afraid for the new Order. This premature scattering turned all plans upside down, and it looked as though Dominic was going to ruin all his work; yet to every objection Dominic replied calmly, "Don't oppose me. I know what I'm doing."

Here was the true character of the man: a contemplative who pondered every problem for long hours in prayer; a man of a single idea slowly realised and put into effect; but when the moment for action came, a man of unusual force. Ten years' silence in study at Palencia, ten years' prayer and meditation at Osma, and ten years' experience of the Albigenses: after these thirty years of meditation and reflection, he founded and brought his Order to fruition in the six remaining years of his life. Step by step, in a series of utterly confident decisions, he changed the Preachers of Toulouse into a world-wide Order. When he died, scarcely four years after the dispersal, he bequeathed to the Church a fully fledged apostolic Order, firmly established in the Universities of Paris and Bologna, strongly supported at Rome by the Pope himself through Dominic's profound influence; it was fitted out with a complete and vigorous set of laws, and had already spread into eleven provinces and about thirty-two convents. And, as if to mark the important step taken in the dispersal, the name of the Order was changed to the one it has held ever since. In the first bull that Dominic received from the Pope after this, the official title was recognised: "the Order of Friars Preachers".

On the 15th of August 1217 the dispersal began. Seven men went to the University of Paris, travelling in two groups to facilitate begging. Their leader was Brother Matthew of France, an older priest than the others, who himself came from the Paris district. Their task was to found a convent, study and "advertise" the Order with the help of the bull of foundation. Most of the parties, like this, went to the theological centres of Christendom.

Dominic did not forget his own country; four of the brethren went, two by two, to Spain. Two or three others stayed at St Romain, all citizens of Toulouse; the same number stayed at Prouille. Dominic himself and a companion set out for Rome a little later. On the feast of the Assumption, 1217, the Dominican Order cast off and set sail on their voyage of discovery round the world.

When the last party had taken their leave of him, Dominic found himself once again alone. With his own hands he had removed the life from his beloved convent of St Romain: the robust singing of office in choir, the comings and goings on preaching tours, and the presence, silent, yet full of life, of the brethren studying in their cells. He must have asked himself whether he was justified in his action, whether he was guilty of presumption, whether he really was acting for the love of God alone.

He shut his eyes and pictured himself once again in St Peter's at the Vatican, completely bowled over, as always, by the sight of the Universal Church: the legates, officers, messengers, bishops from all over the world, collected in council and discussing the problems and urgent needs of souls. And deep in his heart he heard once again the words of the two Apostles who had appeared to him and encouraged him to send out the brethren to convert the world, saying: "Go and preach."

THE SPREAD OF THE ORDER (1217)

Notes on the four plates that follow:

118 "SOW GOOD SEED AND IT BEARS FRUIT: STORE IT AND IT
ROTS"

This was the comment of the chronicler Peter Ferrand on St Dominic's action.

119 SENDING OUT THE BRETHREN

When he scattered the brethren, Dominic did not simply send them to all quarters of the world; in a manner he was conferring upon them a mission from the Church herself. The master of the preachers had such power, and this is signified by the giving of the book in the bas-relief on the tomb at Bologna.

120 SAINT DOMINIC'S STAFF

Relic preserved in the convent at Bologna. The fifteenth-century inscription reads: *De ferula sancti Dominici patriarche*. This staff shaped like a T can also be seen in the miniature (fig. 117).

121 TWO BY TWO THROUGHOUT THE WORLD

The brethren parted from one another sadly, and left their beloved cloister at St Romain to face an unknown future.

[62]

ON arriving at Rome in February 1218 Dominic immediately set to work. He made contact with the Curia and received the first bulls of approbation from the Pope; these would give entry to all the dioceses. At the same time he planned future foundations and works for the Order. He recruited a number of new men and, one after another, he sent four of them to make a foundation in the University of Bologna. Meanwhile news, sometimes good, sometimes disturbing, began to reach his ears about the brethren he had scattered over the Church, and in May he set out to visit them all and settle their problems on the spot.

He visited Bologna first, then Prouille where, with the help of a document brought from the Holy See, he set up a second convent of Preachers, an exact copy of St Romain. He went on down to Spain; there two of the brethren he had sent were already returning, unable to achieve anything. He hurried on to look at the work of two others who were preaching up and down the middle of the peninsula. Perhaps Dominic also hastened with desire to see his native land again after thirteen years.

The records of his movements around this time are not clear, and it is only at Talamanca in November 1218 that we find him again for certain. He was visiting the head of the province, the celebrated archbishop of Toledo, Rodrigo Ximenes de Rada. He had succeeded Diego in Osma and had been Dominic's bishop from 1208 till 1210. Rodrigo received Dominic with such enthusiasm that the remainder of his visit to Spain was taken up with business in Rodrigo's diocese. He ratified the gift to the Order of a house by a priest from Brihuega, through which Dominic had presumably passed on his travels. He also passed through Guadalajara, where his followers had suffered severe disappointments. Finally in December he reached Madrid.

Peter of Madrid, one of two fine preachers sent out by Dominic, had travelled a great deal in his native land. One foundation was being planned in the country, and another house was becoming a centre for religious young women, and Dominic admitted them to vows. Two years later, the situation

[63]

was reversed; the women were keeping house, and it had become a place of rest and recreation for the preaching brethren, after the fashion of Prouille in earlier years. Towards Christmas Dominic was in Segovia where he preached, was an inspiration to everyone, and founded the first Dominican house in Spain.

He set out again northwards, and presumably as he crossed the valley of the Duero, he passed through Caleruega and Osma. We next hear of him in Toulouse in May 1219, from where he sent men to make foundations at Montpellier and perhaps at Lyons. Then taking the road of St James through Rocamadour and Orléans, he made for Paris.

LAST VISIT TO SPAIN (1218–1219)

Notes on the four plates that follow:

122 BRIHUEGA

This little town is situated to the east of the road from Saragossa to Alcala and Toledo. Here are several romanesque churches visited by St Dominic, such as the chapel of St Michael whose priest bequeathed a house to "the Order of Preaching".

123 GUADALAJARA

On the high-road, a little south-west of Brihuega. Here new recruits received by Dominic lost heart, and nearly all deserted; only brother Adam and two lay-brothers remained. Dominic saw them already swallowed up in hell, but his prayer brought them back again.

124 RELIC OF DOMINIC'S CLOTHING

A story from the middle of the thirteenth century tells how a woman came by a piece of coarse material which Dominic wore as a hair-shirt. This relic was first given to the convent at Segovia, and eventually came into the possession of the Cistercians of Las Huelgas at Valladolid. Here is a piece of the material, which is still venerated.

125 A CORNER OF SEGOVIA NEAR THE CONVENT FOUNDED BY DOMINIC

This stairway leading to the romanesque church of St Stephen is close to St Cyprian's gate beyond which lies the Dominican house.

[64]

4

PARIS welcomed Dominic with all the loveliness of spring. Dominic was probably less sensitive to the beauty of nature than to the sight of the thousands of students drinking at the well-springs of truth and never thinking to pass on their knowledge to thirsting Christendom. "Sow good seed and it bears fruit: store it and it rots." As Dominic passed through the Porte d'Orléans, he came to the hostel of St Jacques. Here was the convent of the preachers: thirty friars welcomed him affectionately; Brother Matthew, recently come from Toulouse with six companions, was the head of the community.

Life had not been easy since the autumn of 1217. At first they had lodged in a hostel which they had to rent near Notre-Dame, and they had found great difficulty in obtaining a hearing. People were amazed at their poverty, and one would have expected them to welcome their preaching, for Paris was the centre of orthodoxy. But the Church, led by the archbishop, ignored their existence, and the Canons of Notre-Dame forbade their performing the liturgy in church. Still, a considerable number of young clerics joined their ranks, and a Master of Theology from the University taught them in their own house.

Dominic had just returned from Rome. He had brought from Pope Honorius urgent letters to the masters of the University, which persuaded them to give the Dominicans the hostel beside the church of St Jacques. Dominic took charge of the painful dispute with the Canons of the cathedral, forerunner of many similar ones in years to come. The fact was that, if the Dominicans had a church of their own, the faithful would attend it and fail to make their offerings to the parish coffers. Dominic pointed out that a religious revival, as a result of popular gospel preaching, would in the end benefit the whole Church in Paris, but his argument was fruitless. With Matthew he decided on several missions for the brethren to found new convents at Orléans, Limoges, Poitiers.

Since he knew no French, Dominic could not preach in public but addressed the students about the spiritual life. He told them how at Rome in the previous year Our Lady had miraculously brought Master Reginald, the dean of Saint-Aignan at Orléans, into the Order. A young Master of Arts and Bachelor of Theology listened to this story with close attention. He was Jordan of Saxony, who was soon to become a follower of Dominic and eventually his successor as head of the Order.

PARIS (1219)

Notes on the four plates that follow:

126 THE PROFESSION OF REGINALD IN THE HANDS OF DOMINIC
Bas-relief on the tomb at Bologna.

127 SEAL OF THE UNIVERSITY OF PARIS

128 TEACHING THEOLOGY IN PARIS
St Dominic sent the young brethren to Paris to study. They numbered seven in 1217, thirty in 1219, and one hundred and twenty by 1224. From 1218 onwards they received University tuition. In 1221 the convent was affiliated to the University by a kind of contract.

129 JORDAN OF SAXONY
Jordan, a theological student at Paris, entered St Jacques on the 11th of February 1220. On the 30th of May 1221 he became Provincial of Lombardy, and a few months later succeeded St Dominic.

[66]

B° IORDANVS   II MAGR ORDI
D'ALAMAIA

WHEN Dominic reached Bologna in August 1219, he was greeted with loving veneration by an enormous community. These men had joined the Order as a result of the work of Reginald, whom Dominic had sent here from Rome in 1218 as his own personal representative, and who had fully proved his worth. He had been Professor of Canon Law in the University of Paris and had occupied a high position in the Church at Orléans, but no kind of ecclesiastical success would ever satisfy his ambitions, which were of a different kind. He was eaten up with zeal for spreading the Gospel. When he embraced a life of evangelical poverty, these great energies were released, and he himself was transformed with happiness. From then on, his whole time was taken up in preaching. "His eloquence," says one hearer, "was like a fierce flame, and his words like burning embers to set the hearts of his hearers on fire. Few people had sufficient stubbornness of heart to withstand him. Bologna was ablaze; it seemed that another Elias had come on earth. Thus Master Reginald received numerous Bolognese into the Order."

Dominic was astonished, for he had not expected such a transformation. The previous spring he had left behind at Bologna a handful of preachers who occupied a poor hostel near the church of Santa Maria della Mascarella, unknown and living in a state of poverty that bordered on destitution. Now he found a new priory settled in the church of St Nicolas, for all the clergy of this church had themselves become Dominicans. The community included three Masters from the University, either canon lawyers or philosophers, another University Master who was not yet a priest but had taken a vow and had become part of the household; there were mature experienced priests and young enthusiastic students. All these men had been trained in the discipline of Christ by Master Reginald with love and happiness. Dominic's own happiness was now boundless, for with such men there was no limit to the work that could be undertaken.

Immediately he decided to give the north of Italy the evangelisation it so much needed. Dissension, heresy, ignorance, usury and civil war were as widespread here as in the South of France. He planned to found a network of convents with the great number of excellent friars that were here to hand. Bergamo, Florence, Verona, Milan came into being in a few months; Piacenza and Brescia were established within two years; then Faenza and Parma. In the early years Lombardy was to be the chief Dominican Province in Italy, and from here the Order began immediately to spread to Hungary, Germany and Scandinavia. From now on, Dominic planned to make Bologna his home and never left it except to visit Rome. He returned to Bologna to die, and his body still rests there.

It was at Bologna that he finally organised the Order and laid down the first laws. In 1216 he had settled the day-to-day routine of the Order's life, but a permanent constitution was still to be drawn up. Bologna was the ideal place for this task, for its University was the greatest Christian centre of the study of Law, and already several of the dons of the University had joined the Order. So in 1220 and 1221 the Dominican Constitution was framed here.

Meanwhile, however, Dominic had first to settle one vital principle which should give the Order a distinctive character. It was a matter he had pondered for many months, for in 1215 it had been impossible to see so far ahead. Now his mind was made up, and when Brother Rudolph, the procurator at Bologna, proudly laid before him the deeds of some property recently given to the brethren by a friend of the Order, Dominic tore them up. In 1215, the preachers had taken vows of poverty, according to which they were to have no property but only endowments. Now Dominic went a step further and declared that the Order should have nothing more than daily alms. If a priory had enough to live on for the day, they were not to accept or seek anything more. "The morrow will be solicitous for itself. Sufficient for the day is the evil thereof" (Matt. 6:34). That was the principle of evangelical poverty.

In 1215, Dominic had not yet realised that a community with its novices, its students and its sick could in fact survive on this rule, and he had accepted the regular income allotted by the diocese of Toulouse from its funds for the poor. But since then, his experience in Spain, Toulouse, Paris and Bologna had taught him differently, and he had seen a new spirit grow up in the Order which the Constitutions were to endorse; this was the principle of absolute poverty applied not only to individual preachers on their journeys but to the priories where they lived. This meant complete abandonment to the daily dispositions of Divine Providence.

From this day forward, the people became familiar with the sight of two Dominicans, the "questors", walking the streets of the town or the district around the priory, begging the community's daily bread. Of course this involved additional hardship, but it instilled in the brethren a spirit of absolute detachment, complete confidence in God, and an even greater trust in the supernatural. Brother Rudolph, the procurator at Bologna in these years, relates, "Whenever there was no bread or wine or anything else left in the priory, I would go to Brother Dominic and say to him, 'We have no more bread—or wine', and he would say to me, 'Go and pray and God will provide'. I would go to church to pray, generally followed by Brother Dominic, and God always saw to it that we got enough to eat."

Dominic himself begged like everyone else; he had been doing so for fourteen years. An eye-witness has left us a touching picture of how, on one occasion in the village of Dugliolo, when a man gave him a whole loaf, Dominic went down on his knees in humility and gratitude to receive it.

While he was building up the character of this community by his precept and example, Dominic took a step which gave him great pain: he sent Reginald away from the priory he had founded, to stir up the people in Paris as he had done in Bologna. Dominic himself set off for Rome.

BOLOGNA (1219)

Notes on the five plates that follow:

130 THE MIRACLE OF THE LOAVES AT SANTA MARIA DELLA MASCARELLA, BOLOGNA

The first brethren to arrive in Bologna in the winter of 1218 experienced abject poverty in the little church of Santa Maria della Mascarella. Some boards are still preserved in the church which they used for a table, and on which someone has subsequently depicted the miracle of the loaves of bread. One day, when they had received nothing from their begging, Dominic nevertheless told them to go to the refectory. When they had said grace, two strange young men entered and served bread to all the brethren. The procurator of the time, Brother Buonviso, says that the event, which he himself witnessed, took place not at Santa Maria but at Saint Nicolas.

131 SAINT DOMINIC'S KNIFE

Relic preserved by the discalced Carmelites at Florence. Dominic and the brethren did in fact carry such knives with them (cf. fig. 37).

132 THE *VENIA*

Traditional monastic gesture of humility. The first Dominican constitutions say: "The novice master shall teach the novices to make the *venia* in chapter and wherever they receive rebuke".

133 CLOTHING OF A NOVICE BY SAINT DOMINIC

Fresco from the Spanish chapel of Santa Maria Novella in Florence. When Dominic gave the habit, he usually promised to those who received it "the bread of life and the water of heaven". He would also say, "I am giving you arms with which you can fight the devil for the whole of your life."

134 THE TORN TITLE DEEDS

By this symbolic action Dominic rendered his Order completely mendicant.

[70]

Gladius, quo usus fuit S. Dominicus Praedicator; Pater

DOMINIC was already known at the papal court which at this time was at Viterbo. Chief among the Cardinals who were now friends and intimates rather than official protectors was Ugolino, promoter of new religious foundations and papal legate in Tuscany and Lombardy. As he had done before in 1217, he obtained for Dominic audience and favour with the Pope; but a new friend, William of Sabina, head of the chancellery, did even more. Innumerable papal letters and encyclicals began to commend the work of the Dominicans to the bishops and the faithful, and it was for these that William was largely responsible. These letters gave one endorsement after another to the work of the Friars Preachers: they recalled the pronouncements of the Lateran Council on preaching, and thus put the Dominicans in the central tradition of the Church's teaching; they emphasised the importance of evangelical poverty for making their ministry and preaching effective; they pin-pointed the particular power that their work had exerted over places where heresy had run wild. Privileges were bestowed, to assist their work and their own sanctification, and to protect them against temptations; indulgences were granted, approving the generosity of their ministry and their adoption of uncompromising mendicancy. Orders were issued to protect them against opposition, to give them special powers and help them through difficulties. And finally letters of thanks to the overlords, towns and convents which had received the Preachers well, pointing out that it was the Church herself that had been received in their person.

The Pope held a high opinion of Dominic, and as his trust in him grew, it was reflected in the letters and bulls that issued from the chancellery. He was an older man than Innocent III and less amenable, but he carried on his predecessor's policy and took a special interest in the care of souls and in missionary work in the distant lands of Christendom. Because of this he entrusted two tasks to Dominic.

The first was the reform of some nuns in Rome, a task which Dominic was required to tackle immediately while he was spending a few weeks there at the end of the year. The plan for the second task he took back to Bologna with him in May 1220: he was to organise a papal mission to northern Italy on the same lines as the mission to the Albigenses. The Cistercians had undertaken the Albigensian mission; the Dominicans were now asked to undertake the Italian one, and this indicated the lines of Papal policy for the future.

THE PAPAL COURT

Notes on the four plates that follow:

135 VERANDAH OF THE PAPAL PALACE AT VITERBO

136 ONE OF THE PAPAL BULLS GIVEN TO THE PREACHERS

It deals with the privilege of a portable altar which was granted on the 6th of May 1221. The preachers could not always find a blessed church in which to establish their convents, and according to the liturgical ideas of the time this prevented them offering Mass or even singing office near at hand. Thus they were compelled to go round the town hunting for a suitable place. This privilege overcame the difficulty, and allowed them to set up portable altars in their own houses.

137 POPE HONORIUS III (1216–1227)

Detail from a fresco by Giotto in the basilica of St Francis at Assisi.

138 DOMINIC AND FRANCIS EMBRACE

The meeting between Dominic and Francis only took place in the winter of 1221 in the home of Cardinal Ugolino at Rome. According to Thomas of Celano, they planned together to beg Ugolino not to seek candidates for bishoprics from among their brethren. The memory of this meeting has been cherished in both Orders. It is frequently recalled to calm those troubles that are bound to come from healthy rivalry between two Orders so alike.

[72]

Honorius eps seruus seruorum dei. Dilectis filijs fratribus de ordine predicatorum salut et aplicam ben. Postulastis a nobis ut cum extra ciuitates et villas frequentius eius tatis nec uobis expediat per huiusmodi loca discurrere pro diuinis officijs audiendis celebrandi uobis ubi conuentus de ordine uestro fuerit super altare portatile licentiam preberemus. Nos autem uestris postulationibus inclinati concedimus sine iuris preiudicio alieni. Dat Lateran .iij. Non maij. Pontificatus nostri Anno Quinto.

FIRST GENERAL CHAPTER AT BOLOGNA (1220)

On Whit Sunday, the 17th of May 1220, the priory at Bologna was swarming with life. Thirty delegates had come at the bidding of Dominic from Spain, Provence, France, Lombardy, Hungary and Rome. This was the first general chapter of the Order, in which Dominic together with his brethren was to fashion, as he had in a measure done in 1216, the laws and constitution of the Dominican Order. From the outset, Dominic tried to put himself in the background and persuade another brother to conduct the meeting. When this proved impossible, he secured the election of four "diffinitors", or representatives, who would conduct the business of the meeting with him.

The work done at this first general chapter was sound, balanced and lasting, for the main lines of Dominican law which were set down here still operate to-day with little or no change after seven hundred years. The Order is established in independent priories. The general chapter, made up of representatives of the whole Order, alone has the power to make laws. The head of the Order—soon to be named Master General—has full executive power, and in virtue of that, members of the Order make their vows directly to him. While the chapter lasts, it governs together with the Master General.

The noviciate was also the object of legislation in 1220, for its duration had not yet been fixed at one year. The chapter legislated for the training of students, the training and choice of preachers and the organising of preaching. The apostolic life was confirmed with emphasis on the mendicant character of the Order: no property; no revenues; acquiring and using money was forbidden, as was the use of horses.

As the chapter pursued its business, the text of the constitutions was gradually developed. If Dominic did not actually edit the text, he inspired it intimately. Some of the finer key phrases come directly from him, and the charter of customs and observances of 1216 is closely bound up with the text of the constitutions of 1220. They make up a book of customs in two parts, both fired by one spirit, the spirit of the gospels and the following of the Apostles.

[73]

The representatives dispersed from the general chapter, and returned to their own priories, many of them far distant, to tell their brethren stories of touching reunions and of the inspiring sight of a full-grown Order so different from the little community of Saint Romain which had scattered over the world less than three years previously; they also brought back with them the text of the constitutions, where each of them could find perfectly mirrored and detailed the ideal he was to aim at in his state of life or his office in the Order.

First, as to the whole Order. "Since our rule bids us have one mind and one heart in the Lord, it is only fitting that, living by the same rule and vows, we should be so united in the observance of our religious life that the harmony in our hearts is reflected in the uniformity of our manners; . . . and we should fear lest the smallest neglect of detail should lead to a decline.

"But in this matter the superior has the power to dispense the brethren whenever he sees fit, especially if the observance of the letter of the law should hinder study, preaching or the saving of souls, for it must be borne in mind that our Order was from the start dedicated to preaching and the saving of souls, and our studies should fit us to be of use to our neighbour with all our energies and zeal."

The novices. "They are to learn from their master humility of soul and body, to go frequently to confession with utter simplicity and honesty, to live without any possessions, to set aside their own wishes and practise absolute obedience. . . . He shall teach them such devotion to study that night and day, at home or abroad, they shall always be occupied in reading or meditating, and shall acquire the habit of learning by heart as much as possible. . . . He will teach them also the zeal they should show in preaching when their time is come."

The students. "If it seems good, a place shall be set aside for them where, in the evening after lessons and disputations, and in their other free time, they can meet with their master and put to him their questions and problems. While one of them is putting his questions or objections, the rest shall keep silence and not interrupt the speaker. And if the questioner, either in putting his questions or making answers, shall behave rudely, noisily, shrilly or roughly, the senior, whoever he is, shall rebuke him on the spot. A private cell shall

[74]

not be given to all the students, but only to those who the master judges can profit by it. In their cells those who wish can study, write, pray, sleep and sit up at night for the purpose of study."

The preachers. "Those who can preach, when they set out on their journeys, shall be given the companion whom the prior considers suitable to their character and dignity. When they have received the blessing, they shall go and behave like men who are seeking to save their own souls and those of their neighbours. They will go in a religious spirit like the men of the gospels walking in the footsteps of their Master, speaking only to God or about God between themselves or with their neighbours, and avoiding the company of unsuitable people. When they are about the business of preaching, or travelling for other purposes, they shall carry no gold, silver or other money, and they shall receive no gifts except food and clothing and other necessary objects such as books. Those who are set to preach or study shall have no administrative responsibilities, in order to be entirely free to carry out the spiritual ministry given in their charge; unless, of course, it happens that no one else can be found to carry out these administrative duties, for it is not a bad thing that we should all from time to time be occupied with the routine needs of daily life."

FIRST GENERAL CHAPTER AT BOLOGNA (1220)

The four pictures that follow illustrate community life in one of the original Dominican houses, the priory of St Maximin (Var), built by Robert of Naples at the beginning of the fourteenth century. Actually these lofty gothic rooms are very different from the mean structures at St Nicolas in Bologna which were so low that the procurator wanted to raise the ceilings by an arm's length. When Dominic heard of it he stopped the work, and with tears in his eyes said he did not want to see his brethren living in palaces!

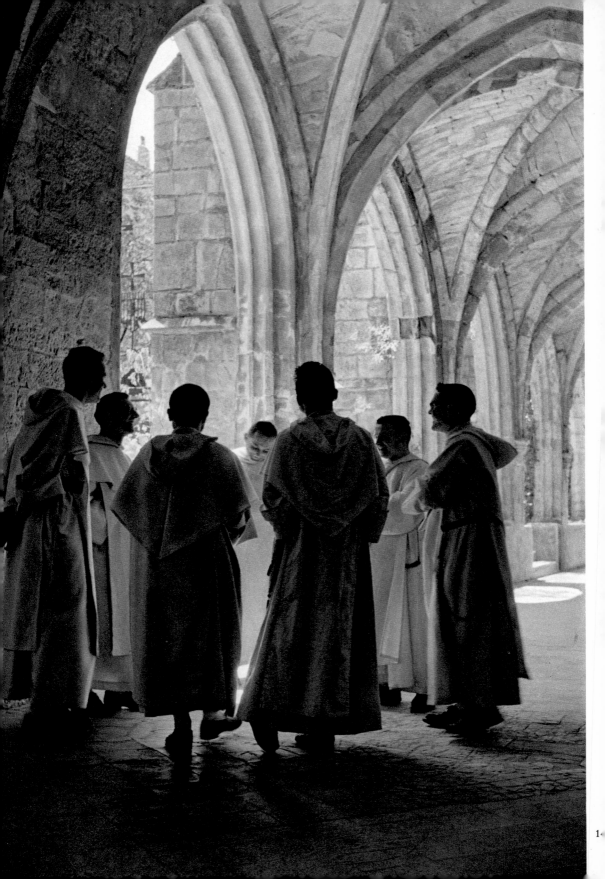

SAN SISTO AND SANTA SABINA

THE story of San Sisto is an essential part of the picture of St Dominic; it is worth many other stories of questionable importance which do not take us so directly to the heart of the man. About 1220 St Dominic came across the ancient monasteries of Santa Maria in Tempulo and Santa Bibiana, and other houses in a state of material and spiritual dilapidation. The Pope entrusted him with the task of restoring these communities and setting up the Sisters in a new house, for which purpose he gave him the old church of San Sisto. During the winter of 1220, Dominic established some of the brethren there to restore the building and at the end of the year he himself returned there. Then, in the intervals of an intense preaching campaign in the city, he devoted part of his time to transferring the communities.

On Ash Wednesday, the 24th of February 1221, he received the vows of the Sisters in their new church; they accepted the charge and, for the time being, he enclosed them in the monastery. Throughout that Lent he gave them instructions in the formation of their new life. Sometimes he was so busy that he could not come to them until night. The Sisters waited patiently. One night they had all gone to bed when the bell rang, announcing his arrival. They got up and found Dominic there with his companions. As the conference went on and they grew tired, Dominic sent for a vessel of wine to restore their spirits; the wine was passed round first to the Fathers and then to the Sisters. Everyone drank, and yet the wine grew no less, whereupon Dominic said with a smile, "Don't be afraid; drink your fill, Sisters."

After Easter, the brethren, who had become a real community, took up residence in the basilica of Santa Sabina, which was the family property of Pope Honorius. Two Sisters had come from Prouille, and other nuns from Rome had joined the convent. Between the 15th and 25th of April sixty-one religious entered San Sisto. The next night Dominic and two Cardinals marched barefoot by the light of torches, carrying the picture of Our Lady from the monastery in Tempulo. Earlier this picture had miraculously returned to its old home on its own, and it was believed that the Sisters would go back to their old convent if this happened again. But the picture stayed with St Dominic; so did the Sisters.

SAN SISTO AND SANTA SABINA

Notes on the eight plates that follow:

143 SAN SISTO VECCHIO

The old fifth-century church is underground. The present church was built in the middle ages above it.

144 GRILLE IN THE PARLOUR OF SAN SISTO

This grille from the convent of San Domenico e Sisto has been taken to Monte Mario and is said to have come originally from San Sisto Vecchio, but it is entirely modern in construction.

145 THE "ACHEROPITE" PICTURE FROM SAN SISTO

This is the Byzantine painting of the high middle ages which the Sisters of San Sisto have carefully preserved. It is presumably the traditional picture of Our Lady sketched by St Luke and painted by angels without the assistance of human hands.

146 YOUNG NAPOLEON RESTORED TO LIFE

This young man, a close relation of Cardinal Stephen of Fossanova who was working with Dominic on the re-settlement of the nuns, fell off his horse. "He looked half-dead, perhaps he was really dead," says one witness. "Dominic had the young man carried into a closed room, and by the power of his prayers alone brought him back to life and led him out in the presence of everyone, safe and sound."

147 THE "ASINARIA" GATE AND THE RECLUSE

On his way to San Sisto, Dominic used to stop and talk to a recluse, whom he cured of a loathsome disease. She lived opposite a gate of the city, probably this "porta asinaria".

148 LA *ROCCA* SAVELLI

Pope Honorius III, a member of the Savelli family, had this castle or *rocca* at the top of the Aventine restored. The basilica of Santa Sabina, where the brethren from San Sisto were housed, formed part of the buildings.

149 INTERIOR OF THE BASILICA OF SANTA SABINA

A jewel of fifth-century Christian art, which Honorius gave to the Dominicans.

150 MASS AT SANTA SABINA

SECOND GENERAL CHAPTER AND DEATH AT BOLOGNA

FOR the sixth time Dominic left Rome, travelling on foot as usual. All along the way communities welcomed him with open arms, at Siena, Florence and so on; and a great consolation this was to him, for after years of ministration and unbroken night-watches he was worn out; his austerities had ruined his health. Nevertheless he still treated himself harshly and would not consider cutting down his work. Eventually he reached Bologna at the end of May.

At Whitsuntide the Order held its second general chapter there, and several enactments had to be made for setting up the territorial unit known as a province. Five such provinces were founded and priors provincial assigned to them: Spain, Provence, France, Lombardy and Rome. In addition, priories had been founded, or men were on the spot ready to found them, in six other countries: England, Germany, Hungary, Dacia (modern Scandinavia), Poland and Greece.

Ever since 1205, Dominic had hoped to devote his own life to converting the pagans, but the mission to northern Italy and the final organisation of the Order had completely exhausted his energies and he was compelled to abandon the idea. But if he could not undertake the work himself, he could see that it was done by the men he sent to the North and East, and so he despatched a formal order to the brethren in Hungary to tackle the savage Cuman Tartars.

Then, together with Cardinal Ugolino, the papal legate for northern Italy, he resumed the great preaching project that he had conducted from spring to autumn in the previous year. For Dominic the settlement of the Preachers was not just a routine task; it shared the character of direct evangelisation. He had served his Master well, and the time was now come for him to lay down his arms: he no longer had the power to preach, and death was at hand. But even death itself, as the eye-witnesses tell us, showed forth his great heart. His own character, like his great apostolic schemes, matured only slowly but steadily, so that it was finally in the very moment of his death that the whole splendour of the man was to be seen.

Ventura, the prior of Verona, tells us: "Towards the end of July Blessed Dominic returned from the court of Cardinal Ugolino . . . which at that time, I believe, was at Venice. Dominic was worn out, for the heat had been suffocating. Yet in spite of his great weariness, he spent the best part of the night discussing the business of the Order with Brother Rudolph and myself (I had just been made prior). Rudolph, being very tired himself, urged Dominic to retire to rest and not to rise for Matins, but he would not, and went to the church where he spent the night in prayer and assisted at Matins, as I myself and the brethren can witness. After Matins the brethren told me he was suffering from a headache; at the same time there set in the sickness [dysentery] which was eventually to kill him. Though he was compelled to lie down, he refused to use a bed and lay only on a woollen sack. He called the novices to him, and comforted and encouraged them with sweet enthusiastic words. He accepted this illness, as he had accepted all the others, with immense patience; he never complained or moaned, but always smiled and was full of joy.

"As the fever mounted, we had him transferred to Santa Maria del Monte where the air was healthier. When he thought he was dying, he called me to him with the brethren; about twenty of us came, and there as he lay he began to speak to us. He gave us a beautiful and most moving sermon, finer than anything I had ever heard him preach.

"I think it was at this point that someone gave him Extreme Unction. While this was going on, I was told that the priest in charge of Santa Maria del Monte was claiming that, if Dominic died there, he would have to be buried there. I told him this. 'God forbid', he said, 'that I should be buried anywhere except beneath the feet of my brethren. Carry me out on to the road so that I may die there, and then you can bury me in your own church.' The brethren lifted him up and carried him to the church of Saint Nicolas in Bologna, terrified lest he should die on the way. [There they placed him in the cell of Brother Moneta because he had none of his own.]

"When he had been there for about an hour, I was summoned and he said to me, 'Get ready, now'. I got everything ready with the brethren to recite the solemn prayers for the departing soul, but when we were all gathered round him he said, 'Wait a while'. [Brother Rudolph supported his head on his arm, and with a towel wiped away the death-sweat from his face.] About this time I said to him, 'Father, you know in what grief and desolation you are leaving us; remember us in the presence of the Lord'. Brother Dominic raised his eyes and his hands towards heaven and said, 'Holy Father, you know that I have always tried with all my power to do your will, and I have kept and protected those you gave me. Now in my turn I give them back to you; do you keep and protect them'. The brethren told me that when they commended themselves to him, he replied, 'I shall be of more use and help to you after death than [if I remained alive]'. A few moments later, he said, 'Begin'. We then began the solemn prayers for the departing soul, and from the movement of his lips it seemed that he was saying them with us. He died during the prayers, and we believed that he actually gave back his life to God at the moment when we said the words: 'Come to his assistance, all ye Saints of God; meet him, ye Angels of the Lord; receive his soul and present it to the Most High'.

"I believe it was through the goodness of Divine Providence that Cardinal Ugolino, then bishop of Ostia, and now Pope, happened to arrive at Bologna. With the assistance of the patriarch of Aquileia and many venerable bishops and abbots he himself celebrated the requiem Mass, gave the absolutions and performed the burial, on the feast of St Sixtus (the 6th of August 1221)."

SECOND GENERAL CHAPTER AND DEATH AT BOLOGNA
Notes on the the four plates that follow:

151 CHIARAVALLE DELLA COLOMBA
The Cistercian abbey near Piacenza, which Dominic visited during the Lombardy mission in
the summer of 1220 or 1221. One night, on arriving there after a hard journey and preaching
tour, he gave the community as usual a conference which was an inspiration to them all.

152 THE INTERIOR OF THE ROUND CHURCH OF SANTA MARIA
DEL MONTE, BOLOGNA
When Dominic was dying, he was carried into this romanesque church and laid on the ground
there because the air on the hilltop was more healthy than in Bologna. As he lay dying, surrounded by his brethren, he could pick out in the dim light the tall figures of the Apostles
standing around against the walls waiting to welcome him to heaven.

153 THE HILL OF SANTA MARIA DEL MONTE
Below lies Bologna in a heat-haze. In the heat of August 1221, the humidity aggravated his
sickness violently.

154 DOMINIC DYING AMONG HIS BRETHREN
Foreground of a tableau by Fra Angelico in the church of Jesus of Cortona.

[82]

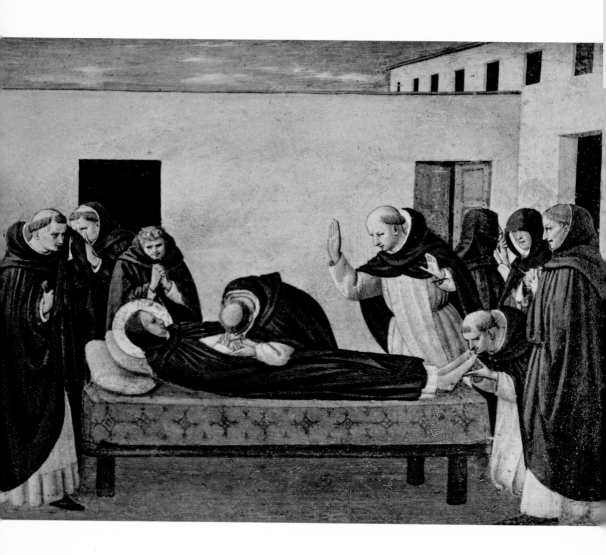

THE CANONISATION

DURING the twelve years that elapsed after the burial of Dominic, public devotion to him grew at a great rate. The Dominican brethren, however, did not take any part in it; indeed, they sought to stifle it. This was not because they were absorbed in their work and study, or because they had forgotten their Father. Ugolino, who was now Pope, rebuked them sternly for what he thought was neglect, but if we are to judge by the sincere devotion with which they bore their witness to Dominic's life at the Canonisation process, it is certain that they had not forgotten him. The truth was that they feared lest, in encouraging the public devotion to their founder, they might appear guilty of seeking wealth and worldly notoriety, the two things of which Dominic had the greatest horror.

They had remained faithful to Dominic's ideals and example, and had practised to the full the statutes and principles he had left them. The ministry of the word spread to the Universities of Paris, Toulouse and Oxford where they taught theology. Priories were continually multiplying, and were strongholds of Christian life and devotion to truth. In the Holy Land, Greece, the marches of Hungary, Poland, Scandinavia, Spain, the brethren had undertaken daring missionary campaigns among the pagans and Ottomans. The great missions, which Dominic had started among the Albigenses and in Lombardy, had grown into huge enterprises in which the Franciscans and secular priests vied with the Dominicans. The Lombardy mission, which for a long time had been hindered by the political and military upsets in the north of Italy, had experienced un-paralleled success from 1230 onwards. In 1233 it started a spiritual and social upheaval which took control of one after another of the great cities of the north, under the title of the "Great Alleluia". It was a revival of Christianity itself, in which the people and their leaders not only broke off all contact with heresy, but stopped all wars and forms of hostility, made peace treaties, reformed the laws of their city-states, made restitution for ill-gotten possessions and banned usury, and finally did penance for their sins and returned to the sacraments and the full spiritual life of the Church. It was a mass return to the practice of religion.

In this atmosphere of religious enthusiasm, the public devotion to St Dominic grew under the stimulus of John of Vicenza, a young Dominican preacher who had roused the whole of Bologna with his popular oratory. The objections of the brethren were overridden, and the Church's permission was sought and received to transfer the remains of the Saint to another tomb. When the tomb was opened, a fragrance of the greatest strength issued from it and reached every single one of the innumerable bystanders. After this, nothing could hold back the popular enthusiasm, and the civil and religious authorities of Bologna applied to Rome to open the process of Canonisation.

The Canonisation, however, which eventually took place under Gregory IX on the 3rd of July 1234, was not simply the outcome of popular enthusiasm. The text of the official proceedings can still be seen: nine moving statements from the brethren of Bologna and thirty from the South of France. Other facts can be found in the little book which Jordan of Saxony edited a short while before the transfer of the remains. Without these evidences we should know very little about the true character of Dominic and his first brethren. They were men dedicated to teaching and administration, who spoke with complete simplicity and a concern for nothing but the truth. Yet they were not lacking in sensitivity. At the end of his little book, Jordan searches through all his memories of his master for what he treasured above all others. It is appropriate that here also, at the end of a collection of photographs of Saint Dominic's life and land, we should set the same treasured picture.

"There was one thing about him," says Jordan, "which was greater than all his miracles. This was the absolute perfection of his very being and the buoyancy and heavenly warmth with which his personality was shot through. This convinced us all that he was bound for heaven. He was utterly serene, except when the sight of another man's misery stirred him deeply and roused his profound pity and fellow-feeling. And just as his glad heart made his countenance cheerful (Prov. 15:13), so the peace of his soul was to be seen in the kindness and joyousness of his looks. When he had decided before God to carry out any project, his spiritual harmony was such that he scarcely ever needed to qualify any decision he had reached after mature thought. And since, as the saying has it, a clear conscience lights up a man's face, it was rare that the light of his countenance fell not on the earth (Job 29:24).

"Through this joy he found it easy to gain everyone's affection; from the very first he easily touched everyone's heart. Wherever he was, travelling with his companions, talking with his hosts and the assembled company, among nobles, princes or prelates, he always spoke salutary words and would tell innumerable stories to lift the hearts of his hearers to love God and shun worldliness. In word and deed he was always a man of the gospel. During the day no one enjoyed more the companionship of his brethren or the friends met on a journey, no one was gayer than he. But at night no one kept watch so assiduously and prayed so fervently in every way. . . . He often wept copiously in the daytime, when he celebrated Mass, which he did frequently, nearly every day; during the night, in his unceasing vigils. . . .

"He embraced all men with his great love, and because he loved the world the world loved him. He made a rule for himself to rejoice with those who rejoice and weep with those who weep (Rom. 12:15). He overflowed with devoted love, and gave himself completely to helping his neighbour and comforting the sad. The frank simplicity of his bearing endeared him to everyone. No trace of pretence or sham ever appeared in his words or behaviour.

"He really loved poverty. He wore the meanest clothes. He was most moderate in his use of food and drink. He set aside all delicacies and took only the simplest food. He exercised supreme control over his body. He drank his wine so diluted that while he satisfied the needs of his body, he never ran the risk of blunting his fine spiritual sensibilities.

"Who will ever come near to the great goodness of this man? We can only wonder at him, and judge the softness of our own age by his fortitude. . . . Let us follow, my dear brothers, the steps of our father as far as we can, and thank God who has given us such a superb leader on the road we must travel; and may God kindle the light and warmth of his holy life once again in us!"

THE CANONISATION
Notes on the five plates that follow:

155 THE TOMB AT BOLOGNA
The work of Nicolas Pisano (1265–1266), embellished in turn by Nicolas of Bari (1470–1494), Alfonso Lombardi and Michelangelo himself.

156 THE CASKET OF CYPRESS WOOD CONTAINING THE RELICS
Later than 1267. In 1943 it was taken out of the tomb and put in a safe place during the last war.

157 A FRAGMENT OF THE SKULL
Kept at Monte Mario.

158 THE SAINT'S BONES
At the time of the removal in 1943 the casket was X-rayed by professors from the University of Bologna in order to examine the bones without opening the casket. Thus it was possible to prove the authenticity of the relics and to make interesting observations about St Dominic's height (5 ft. 5¾ ins.), build, figure, etc.

159 THE OLDEST PORTRAIT OF SAINT DOMINIC
After the school of Guido de Siena. (*The Fogg Art Museum, Harvard University, Cambridge, Mass., U.S.A.*)

[86]

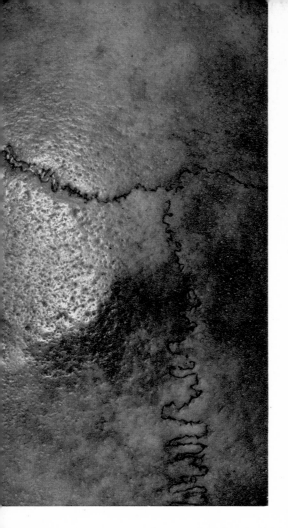
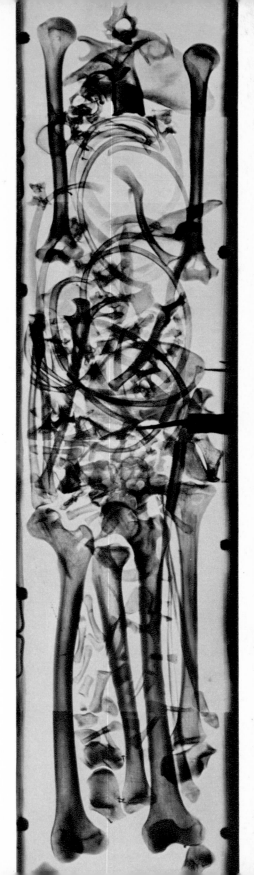

15

INDEX OF ILLUSTRATIONS

(The figures refer to the numbered photographs)